LOOSE ENDS

The Evolution of Consciousness

Part I

Cee Hunt

North Node

CONTENTS

LOOSE ENDS

The Evolution of Consciousness
Part I

W ho W hat W hen W here W hy

This is Part One of The Evolution of Consciousness, based upon the happenings of my own life.

It is meant to capture my frame of mind in the moment the event is happening as opposed to a nostalgic look at my naïve past from my present throne of "wisdom." That being said, I have interlaced pertinent morsels of insight—insight that may not have been readily available to me in the moment—throughout the text as a token to the reader. This is a contradiction, I know, yet contradictions are our nature. So, rather than remedying character flaws and inconsistencies for convenience, I have retained these instances as reminders of the human condition.

Another unavoidable aspect of which are patterns.

We are all destined to repeat patterns.

Some of us eventually gain enough awareness to identify these patterns, but the test that separates the few from the rest is figuring out how to pull ourselves out of these vicious cycles that keep us bound to reliving the same lessons over and over again.

Although this book carries more glimpses of humanity than I can summarize here, these were never my intentions. By default, the nuances of being alive surfaced from my overwhelming intention to write the truth.

My next intention was one of compassion for those who feel lost or alone.

I understand.

I have not penned a self-help book that neatly dilutes the complex nature of our reality because life is not neat nor can it be diluted. LOOSE ENDS is my attempt to revive storytelling as the most effective form of passing down life's greatest mysteries to the next generation.

It is also to show the process of change, proving that it doesn't involve a list of preparations one can master overnight.

Life is one great process of change, woven together with the multiple fibers of our being—memories, events, relationships, mind, rationale, heart, expectations, body, soul, the subconscious, the ego, sexuality, wounds, etc.—forming what seems to be a linear trajectory through time and space.

I only scratch the surface of the magnitude of such an explanation in this book, as if the reader was right there with me, facing the same shattering of former truths (now illusions), negotiating how to open ourselves up to the idea that we are here to determine the meaning of life for ourselves.

Awareness

This book covers 2008 through the first half of 2013. I will not reach the preliminary stage of forgiveness until 2018. Therefore, my perspective of the individuals who impact my journey in this book may come off as skewed. But that is the point.

It takes time for us to see the bigger picture before we can make sense of the intricate lessons facilitated via our connections with others.

I have—with great care and respect—done my best to conceal the identities of said individuals without compromising the integrity of the matter.

If I ever hurt you, or these unearthed memories of our encounters feel unfair, I apologize. My intention with sharing our exchanges is to spread humble seeds of healing. The first stage of which is interacting with the truth.

The answers come from within,
not from without.

Childhood

Tension existed before I knew what it meant.

News of my conception was received the same day my maternal grandmother voiced her desire to take her life.

My mother resented her mother for these selfish antics: tiresome episodes of inflicting harm upon herself that indirectly harmed those that loved her. But the severity of a suicidal statement was not an invitation to prove a point. Rather, it was a timely call to action for my mother to remind her mother that life is bigger than just ourselves.

But how?

My grandmother's neglect for her daughter's feelings—a blindness to the inherited misery reflected back at her—was the unspoken dynamic of their relationship.

Why would it be different this time?

Because, this time, the climax of her hopelessness had perfectly intersected with the unwritten chapter of a grandchild.

I grew up spending the night at this grandmother's house almost every weekend, unaware that the promise of my life became the purpose of hers; one of the many pieces of my environment no one knew how or when would be appropriate to share with me, if ever.

It's thematic content like this that adults presume children cannot understand when, in actuality, it's burrowing deep into our formidable beings, reminding us that we came to help carry the baggage our parents cannot carry alone.

Other such artifacts of my origins that the sands of time slowly but surely revealed consisted of:

• my father's consistent unemployment;
• the magnitude of my mom putting herself through both a bachelor's and doctorate program, during which she completed two pregnancies and one miscarriage;
• my parents' childhoods, both of them emotionally scarred from traumatic situations, which they planned to remedy by doing the opposite of what their parents did to them; and
• whether my parents were really in love with one another or not.

By age six, the seeds of tension from my mother's womb had sprouted through the edges of my heart.

I didn't understand all the *no's* I received when I would ask if I could ride my bike over to another street, if I could play at Sandra's house, or when I tried to close the door to my room in the off-chance a friend wanted to come over to my house and play. Their reasoning usually fell into one of two categories: *Because I said so* or *It isn't safe.*

I had yet to realize that my frustration was not due to their incomplete responses as much as it was the inheritance of their unresolved pain.

I could not see that their overbearing love for me was a justification for the lack of love they received as children. I could not see that I was overprotected because they refused to accept the general lack of control that governs our lives, making me an available outlet for creating a sense of certainty. I could not see the difference between the way the world works and the way my parents were teaching me that the world works. I could not see that the injustice of life is not a reality but, rather, a perspective.

No one was breaking down life in such a way that made sense of the forms of strife that we all experience. No one was deconstructing fear as illogical because no one regarded fear as the force that influenced people to stay within their comfort zones. No one opened up about how they really felt, modeling how our emotions inform the way we interpret our experiences because we were conditioned to view life as predictable and immune to change. Denial reigned supreme.

I was sent to a variation of Christian school from fourth grade through high school.

School was not an intentional sacrifice my parents had made in order to fill my future with opportunity. Instead, it was the place every kid went for the majority of the day, differentiated by uniforms and prayer from the places other kids went.

From the time we were small, teachers trained us to follow the rules, internalizing the duality of bad and good, mean and nice. But once we had learned to read the instructions for ourselves, they stopped smiling, ringing hand-held bells to get our attention, and rewarding us with ice cream parties. Our maturation exposed us to systemically acceptable cruelty; a less guidance, more judgment protocol, challenging our command of cultural paradigms and instilling within us a fear of consequences.

We were inherently changing but had no way of comprehending it beyond our grade in school. Our physical emergence into hormonal living was labeled as "puberty," a bodily becoming diluted into birds-and-bees classes, separated by gender, where parents hovered above a slideshow that ushered us into adolescence. They confirmed that sex did in fact make babies, accompanied by the obligatory warning of the high probability of contracting an STD, and that sex was a sinful act outside the covenant of marriage. This pivotal stage was not a ceremonial rite of passage, an official bestowment of more knowledge and, consequently, more responsibility. Instead, it was a politically correct presentation of our physiology underlined by the religious duty of our school.

A deeper understanding of who we were beyond what we were doing—going to school, extracurricular activities, and friendships—went unexamined.

Okay, yes, facets of our existence were explained, but they existed within a vacuum.

We didn't talk about why we are alive besides that our parents loved one another very much; that God made replicas of himself into human form, whom he also loved very much; and that a sperm and egg had formed a zygote that remained nameless for 9 months until its first contact with the oxygenated atmosphere of the human world.

We weren't taught how to meditate or reflect; rather, we were taught to pray because that's what Jesus did and that's what the Bible teaches us to do.

We weren't encouraged to be curious; rather, our curiosity was controlled by our carefully sculpted curriculum—an apparatus built with the purpose of preparing us for the world, yet that neglected to instill the most crucial lesson of them all.

How to think for ourselves.

One time in sixth grade, I had been talking about sex on the home phone with a boy in my class.

Shortly after hanging up, my mother knocked on the door before entering my room, a yellow legal pad scribbled with notes shone brightly in her hand. She had been on the other line transcribing moments of concern. I wanted to scream, hit her in the face, and make her disappear; but, regardless of my horror, she proceeded to discuss the contents with me, recounting her own horror at some of the things her eleven-year-old daughter had said.

I was already confused and uncomfortable, navigating the murky waters of colloquial conversation with a boy about an unfamiliar topic. My mother's own discomfort with the topic only served to confuse me even more.

I was not allowed to watch PG-13 movies until I was 13. But, regardless of my age, I was required to cover my eyes during any sex scenes. Masturbation was taboo and met with facial expressions that rejected it as an act of shame, painting the range of human experience with judgment before hurriedly covering it up so others wouldn't see.

My heart was hardening.

Every year, I would get invited to travel with my best friend and her family on lavish trips to Aspen or Hawaii but was never allowed to go. So, eventually, my friend gave up asking, and I received postcards and the occasional trinket from her in the mail.

None of it made sense.

Why could I sleep over at this friend's house but not go on vacation with her?

My parents' unconventional approach to my upbringing consumed my focus, blinding me from the other, more obvious aspects of our circumstances.

A life led on the dusty outskirts of the studded realms of gated communities, transported in and out of the safety of illusion by a malfunctioning car. A life with limited exposure to other cultures and environments, rare vacations spent in the doppelgängers Vegas and Palm Springs, where the options were limited to sunbathing and going out to eat. A life of internalized difference from those that surrounded us. My mother did not have a cleaning lady, go shopping at the mall during the week, or get together with other moms for coffee after dropping us off at school. We didn't eat dinner at the table as a family. Instead, we sat on a picnic tablecloth laid on the living room floor. We ate off paper plates while watching TV, my parents sharing their "observations" regarding a person's appearance rather than generating conversation that expanded our concept of what it means to be alive.

Because life was an act.

Most people conducted life on the surface, preoccupied with material things, looking good, and fitting in.

I am talking about the inspiration for The Real Housewives of Orange County and their spawn, my peers.

The invisible boundaries that categorize people hardened as we grew. Limited Too shopping and American Girl parties in elementary school quickly turned into Roxy apparel and surf lessons in middle school until the remnants of our self-designated innocence vanished with the transition into high school. Some forever friends turned into memories because their negligible parental supervision helped them to become the faces of cool—a mask I would only be allowed to admire from afar—leaving only one outlet where I could swim freely.

Basketball. It had rules, expectations and concrete ways of fulfilling the former two. It allowed both parents and children to selectively forget all that we dared not talk about—our insecurities, our worries, and our inequalities—and replaced it with weekend tournaments that elicited the collective goal of victory. Parents went to dinner together and got drunk before games while we roamed the comfort of our Spanish-influenced campus during conference play. Nerves were muffled by iPod headphones and subdued by the companionship of other girls who were working just as hard as me to accomplish the same thing.

Even though *I* could sense taboo subtleties bubbling beneath the surface, without the acknowledgment from others of such things, I had no real way of confirming or denying their existence. Life was what you could see in front of you and that's just the way it was for everyone.

PART ONE:

AMERICA

The Shift

I am sixteen.

My subliminal conditioning at home and school has taught me how to balance upon the thin edge of who I am versus who others are suggesting I be.

I am loud and theatrical because it makes my parents laugh at home and gets me noticed at school. Despite my desperation to be accepted, without the one necessary standard for popularity—my parents' indifference to my whereabouts—I am confined to narrow sanctions off the court. My parental-approved friend group is from basketball, my activity that takes all of my time outside of school is basketball, and my parents will do anything to help me succeed in basketball.

Even though part of me wants to be drinking and taking hits with some former friends and some new ones, basketball is the only harmonious way of distracting myself from that void of exploration. Harmonious because my parents love it and it doesn't afford me the time to indulge in imagining the freedom to be because it is five-thirty p.m. and I still have thirty more minutes of pushing through these hang cleans and wind sprints before I go home to eat and do my homework, and wake up tomorrow to do the same thing all over again.

The first two months of my junior year were more eventful than the first two years of high school combined.

I had not only earned a spot on the varsity basketball team, but after preparing for the season to start, the coach informed me that I would be alternating starting at the guard position with another girl on the team.

My parents somehow afforded replacing my gold Ford Crown Victoria with a pre-owned Mercedes, emphasizing that it was *their* new car that they were letting *me* drive.

Then, in October, a group of friends and I went to a Halloween-themed amusement park where I met my future boyfriend of two years.

The timing of external elements shifting into a more favorable frequency did not strike me as meaningful then. Because no matter how well things seemed to be going, it was a proven fact that my parents would obstruct the flow.

Even at sixteen, they were still regulating whose house I could go to or spend the night at.

"Why don't you trust me?" I would groan.

"It's not that we don't trust you. It's that we don't trust other people."

So I wasn't expecting much when I asked my parents if I could spend the night at Leila's house on one November night. But since my parents had frequent contact with her parents at our basketball games, I was allowed over without a burden of hurdles to jump.

Insert unprecedented surge of invincibility here.

When Leila suggested that we go over to Ginger's that night—a girl in my grade who was notorious for having low-supervision get-togethers—I didn't even flinch.

I was going to ride this wave out even if it crumbled into a bitter end.

There were a few congregations of two or three people strewn throughout, sipping beer out of the bottle like I'd only ever seen adults do.

Leila launched into each group like the social butterfly she was as I stood idly in the center of the living room. For what felt like forever, I was negotiating whether I was destined to be a wallflower for the remainder of the night, until a hand upon my shoulder brought me back to life. It was Ginger, guiding me to the kitchen.

"Hey. So what do you want to drink?"

"Well, what do you have?"

Browsing through the selection, I assumed that any alcohol flavored with watermelon would be my best bet, and I was right. The surprisingly smooth taste of a few Smirnoff Ices catapulted me into an unfamiliar state.

Buckling under my sea legs, I was laughing at a joke told by the fake plant in the living room when Leila approached with urgency.

"Hey. You need to call your parents. They keep calling my mom telling her they need to talk to you."

Shit.

I didn't have cell reception at the house, so they were probably wondering what was going on. I knew I couldn't speak coherently but also knew that not calling them was a sure-fire way of them finding out that I was breaking every rule they had.

I used Leila's phone to call my mom.

"Hey. Why aren't you calling from your phone?"

"Her mom works in Los Angeles."

"What? What do you mean?"

In my brain, I was trying to explain that my friend's phone number had a different area code than ours because of where her mom works, but I had never experienced the potent effects of inebriation before. I didn't know how to keep it together.

"I hate to ask this, but have you been drinking?"

"No."

"Don't lie."

Unable to wriggle out of my mother's omniscience, I surrendered into silence.

"We're coming to get you."

The rest of the night elapsed without much effort or comprehension of the gravity of the situation. We called Leila's older brother to come get us, an inconvenience that went undiscussed because he knew what my parents were like.

We sat in the back of his truck, singing along to our favorite songs just like we did when we were sober, returning to their house a breath before my parents sped into the driveway.

Since I was unable to walk, Leila's brother and my dad carried me out to the car where I gently coiled into the passenger seat. My mom was not with us since someone had to drive my (their) car back home.

I was sending my whole body as much awareness as I could muster, but my eyes were involuntarily shutting as I drifted in and out of consciousness.

"Wake the fuck up, Cee. Your mom is super pissed."

The anesthetic effects of a body stacked full of lead blocked any pangs of guilt he wanted me to feel.

The last thing I remembered was my mom yelling at me to *hold on to the* **goddamn** *toothbrush* after it had slipped out of my hands at least twice, tumbling into the sink.

The next morning, I woke up to my body rejecting itself. With each step down the stairs, coherent nausea wound tighter around my limbs. My mom was in the kitchen with her back to me, fixing something at the counter.

"What are we having for breakfast?"

No sound. No pivot. I wasn't even sure if she was going to respond considering how long she waited to aim her arrow where she could draw the most blood.

"If you're old enough to drink, you're old enough to make your own breakfast."

(Yeah, she seriously said that.)

I stood motionless, awaiting her next move to dictate mine.

"How could you do this? What did we do wrong in teaching you?"

She was crying now, tethered to my gaze just long enough before taking her residual melodrama out on the eggs, each shell exploding on the edge of the bowl.

Thankfully I did not have to endure the waves of tension between my dissatisfying bowl of cereal and my mother's runaway angst because my dad called me into the backyard.

I closed the door behind me as a shovel was thrust into my hand, alluding to the dirt pit behind him.

"You're gonna help me with the sprinkler system today."

The only positive that came out of the sun's brutality that day was the natural purification of my previously virgin lymphatic system. Four hours of sweat stinging my eyes against the lethargic motion of my shovel swing; I wondered when my parents would present me with the new terms of my custody.

M y week-old prize of a car was revoked indefinitely. I was to be driven to and from school by my parents, during which I was forced to read articles on teenage drunk driving accidents they had printed off the internet. As far as free time went, Friday nights at the movies with friends would be replaced with scrubbing cabinets and cleaning the grout behind the toilet with a toothbrush, among other undesirable, laborious tasks. But the punishment with the potential to last forever was cut short by another unexpected occurrence in my life a month later.

I t was our second home game of the season. I launched up for a rebound, jumping backwards at an angle to reach for the ball, when I was pushed from behind and landed straight-legged on my right leg before collapsing to the ground.

Sound extinguished and feeling numbed.

There was a brief blackout before my mind came back online.

Get up!

I pushed myself off the ground, unaware of whether heads had formed a circle staring down upon me or not. Limping as a precaution, I carried myself to the bench. But the respite was brief. The school trainer tapped me on the shoulder, motioning for me to follow him outside to test my knee.

"Alright, jump."

I jumped.

"Now shuffle."

I shuffled in both lateral directions.

"Okay. Now cut."

I ran at a slower pace, planting my right foot. I put all my weight into my right leg before shifting left. I felt a pop. My knee gave way beneath me as my face slapped against the cold ground.

I missed class the next morning for an expedited appointment with an orthopedic surgeon.

His analysis of my knee was brief, almost immediately ordering an MRI and reading the results in the same examination room I had entered a mere hour earlier.

"You have torn the ACL and meniscus in your right knee."

My expression did not change.

"Okay. So what's next?"

"Well, Cee, we are going to have to operate. You probably won't be back on the court for eight to twelve months."

Stable land granulated into sand.

I was trying to keep in mind that, no, I had not just received news of a parent's death nor had I been diagnosed with an incurable disease. But a similar rug of security had been ripped out from underneath me.

My identity.

Aﬅer surgery, I was on crutches for six weeks, immersed in a brief version of what it means to be immobilized.

Such novelty caused my thoughts to swing from the mature plains of empathy before falling back into the childish sand trap of jealousy over my teammates' immunity to such hardship. Envy was to be expected for someone in my position but how did I overcome it beyond screaming and crying from the comfort of my bedroom or dry swallowing it while I sat on the bench during games? Without an immersive routine, I had a surplus of energy and time. Glimmers violently flickering outside the window of my mind were readily apparent, enticing me to interact with territory outside my established bounds. But without anything definitive to compare them to, their presence was meaningless. I yanked the blinds down on their invitation to engage with something that had never been there before because I did not know that these new thoughts and emotions were friendly confirmations of an inner world that only I could see, touch, hear, and feel because I did not know how to interpret pain. The only life I knew was what happens in front of me because that's the only thing teachers, friends, and parents presented as reality. So just because my life currently looked and felt different that did not mean that it would never look and feel the same again.

My dismissal of a cosmic presence catalyzed one of these glimmers, sending a sediment into my consciousness while preparing for the SATs.

It was highly probable that basketball would not determine where I went to college.

I had missed junior year, the most crucial year for recruiters and coaches to determine the select few to add to their already existing collegiate rosters, forcing me to interact with what was in front of me.

Freedom.

It was only a year away.

A confirmed proximity that brought a weight of uncertainty. Maybe freedom isn't what I think it is because life had just radically shown me twice that nothing is as it seems. You can think you have everything, and then one misstep—either by choice or chance—can make it disappear. The outline of the corral I had spent my whole life within crystallized into view. Beyond its borders, reeds of the lush field of choice idyllically blew in the wind. A sign upon one of the posts notified its impending removal.

Graduation date: June 2008.

K nee rehab came and went alongside summer. I had a starting position again as a senior but nothing felt steady. While the majority of my classmates had finally concretized into versions of themselves everyone could understand—stoner, hipster, probably-gonna-be-famous—I no longer knew who or what to be. We were all about to part ways, breaking ties that had grown as deep as appendages over the short course of three years. The confirmation of an end with these people and this place caused me to contract inward, shielding myself from the pain of the inevitable. I was physically present at the football rallies, the dances, and going to the movies but it would have been too much to feel all that these fleeting encounters meant.

Just because I went to the social outings didn't mean I was fully being me.

Who was that?

Without basketball, I was just the loud girl that ran across campus during passing period, surprising random classmates that I could discern from behind with "credit cards" (swiping my hand along someone's clothed butt crack). I was holding onto my hardened exterior of wackiness while slowly letting the internal slack out on

8

all that I did know—the few friends that loved me unconditionally, basketball, and doing well in school—to prepare myself for a place that both terrified and enlivened me.

The freedom of the unknown.

A few weeks prior to receiving my acceptance letters to UC Santa Barbara and UC San Diego, the UC San Diego women's basketball staff reached out to me. Although I was not being recruited, they were offering me the opportunity to train with the team for the summer before walking on in the fall.

Time had pushed me to the edge of the gates where I was awaiting the hand of god to funnel my release into either a world of structure at UC San Diego or a world of partying at UC Santa Barbara. But this higher power did not push me in either direction like they had with my knee. It was up to me. It was up to me to use what I had seen to choose between redeeming the past and temptation.

After considering the former unlikelihood of basketball playing a determining role in my future and the amount of identity upheaval I had already endured without it, I chose UC San Diego.

This selection of a path accelerated time, pushing everything else into the background. I spent my summer driving down to San Diego to train for five hours each day instead of seizing every possible remaining moment with others with whom everything would eventually change anyway. The firm and familiar trail of basketball offered the purpose and direction that depending upon other people could not. My closest friends had not given me any concrete reasons to doubt the strength and malleability of our friendships. It was my inability to be vulnerable that pushed them into a box labeled *past* and put all my emphasis on an external endeavor that I could control.

Saying *goodbye* meant that I accepted that we would no longer be as close as we once were. It meant that I accepted change on every level. It meant that freedom didn't make life easier. Freedom meant letting go of what I think is supposed to happen; a concept that was about to infiltrate every area of my life.

I was not about to leap off the cliff of my youth and float through maturity. I was about to leap off and fall into the depths; an unforeseeable first step on one's unique path to the meaning of life.

Freshman Year

I didn't make the team.

The only closed stall of the women's restroom offered me sanctuary to process the humiliation more than the news itself. Because once I had stopped crying, I did not feel dejected. Every dry blink I took was not to wish away a sore heart. Rather, this second chance at basketball had served as my safe transport into a world I could not fathom as a junior in high school. By trying and failing, the decision I had been too apprehensive to choose then had just been confirmed as the road I must take now.

The archetypal student at UCSD wore a tie-dye t-shirt and cargo shorts and elected to play Xbox 360 from a beanbag chair in their free time.

I needed a community.

A community with social skills and face-to-face extracurricular activities. But the only organization that both boasted and reflected such qualities was Greek life.

So I rushed.

And, by the end of my first month, I was dating a frat boy named Tosh, dressing up in skimpy outfits on Friday and Saturday nights and taking pulls from handles as people cheered by my side.

F or Halloween, I drove up to Santa Barbara with my big sis in
my sorority and two other girls in Greek life.
The road trip ceremoniously opened with the pipe of bud floating
between the tentacles of these counterculture girls to the alternating
tunes of Bay Area rap and punk rock. I passed on each turn,
embarrassed to screw up the proper technique in front of these
intimidating sophomores and juniors. They did not pressure me
nor question me because I was not an equal traveling in the same
stylishly rundown 1990 Jeep Cherokee. I was the token witness to
their nonchalantly cool approach to life.

W e rolled into Isla Vista at around eight p.m. to a foreboding
crime scene. Police cars decorated the streets like Christmas
lights with ambulances scattered throughout, breaking up the string
of black and white with a touch of red.
My eyes widened and my heart sank.

Do people die at this party?

"Hey," I chirped. "Why are there so many police cars here?"
"It's just in case."
My big sis was distracted by looking for any available inch of
curb space to squeeze into.
"Well, then, what's with the ambulances?"
She could hear the worry in my voice, though she would never
say it. She was too nice to sarcastically remark upon another's
weakness.
"Those are drunk tanks. If they find you and you're too drunk,
they put you in there."

I was a hippie, poorly adorned in a last-minute, thrift store purchase—gypsy crop-top—paired with American Eagle Daisy Dukes and a headband across my forehead.

My big sis overshadowed me on all accounts. Perfectly formed breasts accentuated by her tight white dress finished with a pair of children's fairy wings that happened to fit perfectly across her narrowly sculpted back. But I was okay with no one paying attention to me. In her unrelenting attempts to teach me discernment, my mother bird had low-key succeeded. At the very least, I was not looking to get arrested.

We rolled into the first stranger's house of the night. The typical shabby, college rental equipped with the bare essentials juxtaposed by a monument of empty beer cans towering shoulder height next to the trash can in the kitchen. I was waiting for my sis to pour me a shot when someone tapped me on the shoulder. At first glance, it looked like a Russian man cross-dressed as a circus geisha. Once I was launched mid-air in this person's embrace, I realized it was Tosh.

I had not told him where I was, assuming that we would not be able to organize a meeting point along this meta-maze in the dark. How had he found me?

We split off from my big sis and her friends, clutching one another's hands on a blurry cake walk through houses haunted by ghosts inhabiting their owners' drunken bodies. The collective level of debauchery made time feel irrelevant up until it began to rain. Lines of people—hugging their bodies for warmth—swarmed the sidewalks, waiting for a sober angel in a divinely lit car to take them back from where they came.

Tosh randomly took off toward an airport shuttle as it accelerated from a stop sign, hitting the side of the moving van, trailing it until it stopped.

Worry crept back in.

While Tosh was talking to the shuttle driver, his friend, Tony, dressed as the cop from the Village People, was pretending to direct traffic in the middle of the street. Tosh flagged us over, and we hopped into the Toyota minivan, reaching to close the door as the driver hastily sped away.

I slid into the third-row seat next to my sloppy clown before facing forward to notice that our drivers were not professionals. They were two 16-year-old hoodlums.

No one spoke, a silence wound so tight I thought I would die from fear before they got around to shooting me and dumping my body into some remote lake tucked behind the mountains.

The passenger in the front seat didn't turn around, mumbling, "So, where we goin'?"

Tosh, in his attempts to connect with these rogue high schoolers, casually informed them of our preferred destination when it hit me.

Not only was this car ride precarious, but this car ride was leading me to another unknown place.

I was going home with Tosh, someone I had known for only a month, and Tony, who happened to be twenty-five years old and didn't live at this final destination either.

The return of the silence intensified my negative thoughts, so I impulsively blurted the first thing that came to mind.

"Hey. Do you have any Tech N9Ne?

The passenger slowly peered around his left shoulder, taking in the face of the unruly victim before punishing the voice that had spoken out of turn. But then something beautiful happened. He gave me a thug nod, turning around toward the radio. A Tech N9Ne CD was already loaded into his airport shuttle CD player. All he had to do was press play.

The opening to *I'm a Playa* filled the van, and each person in the car was feeling it. Shoulder swaggin' to the rhythm of the song, a curved hand in the air striking each beat, heads slowly bobbing, all in anticipation of the crescendo before the catchy chorus: *I'm a Playa, I'm a Playa.*

Once we arrived at the house, Tosh squelched whatever temporary solace that car ride had surprised me with. **We would be sleeping on the floor in this house of five men, all in their 20s.** He emphasized the luck in the matter rather than the obvious lack of idealism.

I was eighteen, barely covered by damp hippie garb, with a dead Motorola Razor in my pocket. I didn't have the slightest clue as to how Tosh knew these men or how I would handle meeting them in the morning.

This was the place my parents had prevented me from experiencing. The visceral and edgy discomfort associated with uncertainty.

After a night of mediocre slumber, we woke up early and made the hungover trek back to San Diego before class the next morning. The light of day from the car window exposed the mundane nature the dark had fooled me into believing was fear just a mere six hours prior.

The scary older men that lived there?

They were asleep when we arrived and still sleeping when we left.

What my parents had also failed to tell me was that discomfort drives instinct and cultivates trust in unseen forces that are made available to you in the moment.

Tosh was one of the first people to show that to me. A person fluent in instinct. He would've never classified experiences in life as learning things *the hard way* because, for him, that was the only way life allows us to learn anything.

Tosh was two years older than me, born into a broken home of immigrant parents that could barely make ends meet. A fact that felt like fiction. He survived on student loans and the occasional gig catering conferences on campus, and he never complained. The love in his heart was too big. He had not only adopted two rescue pups that smelled like cows, contributing to the already barn-like nature of his apartment, but he had urged one of his best friends from his hometown, Jack, to move to San Diego and share his room with him.

Jack was that misled kid who, without proper guidance, made poor choices, suffering from the exact consequences my parents feared would happen to me. Every time Jack fell, Tosh would pick him up and convince him that it was okay to start over because Jack represented all of their friends back home who were content with never amounting to their potential. Jack's proclivity to spend all of his time and money on drugs was the reason Tosh was never tempted to.

But, when we are young, we haven't lived long enough to realize that some people cannot simply change their perspective by virtue of occupying the same physical space as us. We are inherently born into different perspectives, and the innate way we view the world cannot be removed from the way we absorb new environments. Perspective must be informed by more than just a place. It must be informed by one's willingness to engage in the process of breaking down their surroundings in order to understand them on a different level.

In February, we were drunk at Disneyland for his first fraternity formal.

Paces away from the entrance to the Matterhorn at seven-thirty p.m., sobriety filtered the conversation enough for actual information to be relayed.

"So, where are we going for dinner?"

He looked at me as if to say, *Why would I know that? You're the one who used to live around here,* even though it was Valentine's Day.

That's how I left the scene as I climbed into my mind to locate a logical next step. But clarity had been compromised by a dual conjunctivitis infection that would perpetuate itself for two more weeks since I had stopped taking my antibiotics in order to drink. I had spent the last eight hours underneath the scratchy wool sweater of strangers surrounding me and a boyfriend without a clue. I re-entered reality without a response. I moved away from him against the crowd to the nearest exit, where I began to run. I broke through strings of families connected by a chain of interlocked hands and matching t-shirts, but the distinct feeling of him following me only made me run faster. He trailed me through Disneyland and California Adventure until we reached the Grand California Hotel, where I had made us a reservation just in case he forgot. Not much was accomplished in our incoherent state of cat and mouse beyond a sour dinner absorbing the excess alcohol pooling in our stomachs. And, even though he had been noble enough to pay, we split up a week later.

We took a brief break from talking, but there was still something drawing us together. Which is how I tagged along as his date a few months later for the second fraternity formal that year.

Frat bros traded their Magic Bullet protein shakes for homemade piña coladas while us girls sloppily hung onto their glistening Hawaiian Tropic–lubed bodies, grinding our butts into their pelvic bones, acting like arm candy in a low-budget music video.

We stuffed two Vegas cabanas to the brim with eighty-plus reckless college students, showering ourselves with endless yards of daiquiris as we celebrated our fleeting youth, heavily unaware of everything and everyone else.

I awoke Sunday morning with my pajamas on but without any recollection of the banquet event that I had indubitably attended after the pool party. I was convinced that the reason I blacked out was because I had not eaten, and I shared my reasoning with one of my sorority sisters when I got to her room. It was customary for us to meet up after a long night of intoxication to do some investigative work, flipping through the pictures on her Canon digital camera, putting muddled mental glimpses back together.

"Seriously, Cee? You don't remember eating?"

I shook my head.

"Cee. When you got into the venue, you were running around without shoes on. You see your wristband? Everyone else's was green. You were flagged from the moment we got there. Then, in the buffet line, you used your hands to scoop food from the trays and proceeded to eat like this."

She showed me a picture of myself—the wild child—opening my mouth as wide as could be, shamelessly displaying my unmasticated dinner. I started cracking up, and she echoed the sentiment while selectively scrolling to another picture of Tosh and I grinding on the dance floor.

Drunken words (actions) are sober thoughts, right?

Tosh's altruism and friendship is what had initially drawn me into a romantic relationship with him, but there was an overlooked consistency tearing us apart from the inside out.

He was the first person in my life I was having sex with, and, unless we were drunk, it didn't work.

I didn't talk about it with anyone because not only did I want to save the embarrassment of my boyfriend, but there wasn't anyone I trusted enough to confide in. My mom would have crawled out of her skin upon me voluntarily voicing my choices to drink and fornicate, often at the same time. I had to convince her to let me take birth control by claiming I was having uncontrollable acne. But the truth was that every month before my period, I would convince myself that I was pregnant, even though it was an impossibility since most often he went limp inside me, which was the real problem.

I did not fully understand how sex worked.

The abstinence classes from my private high school did not

explain sexuality nor the basic components of the sexual experience. I did not know how to orgasm. I did not know that pulling out was not as enjoyable as him finishing inside of me, but I also did not want to seem unknowledgeable about things I assumed other people knew all about.

Freshman year was approaching its close, offering one final hoorah at the all-campus spring festival.

I skipped class on Friday to get ready with a few girlfriends from my sorority—coordinating our sorority tank tops with our sorority-branded fanny packs—before boarding the shuttle to a fraternity pre-party. Us four girls carried a squad momentum that extinguished as soon as we opened the door.

Only ten other people were there, half of whom were girls.

We branched off to greet our token acquaintances when I began chatting with Nicole, a girl I had met during rush. It had been about five minutes of *blah blah blah* when I finally referenced her holding two red Solo cups.

"Where'd you get that drink?"

"Oh, here. Someone made this for me, but I don't want it."

And that was the last thing I remembered.

I woke up on my dorm room bed to nightfall outside my window and Tosh's body strewn across the brief remainder of the extra-long twin.

The clock read eight p.m.

What?

How?

A sheet of ripped notebook paper lying by my bed cast a shadow over a large wet spot on the carpet below. The note was from one of my friends, Maria, who had been with me earlier. It said to call her when I woke up.

"Oh my god. I am so glad you're okay."

"What the fuck is going on?"

19

"Here, just come meet me at the field."

I woke up Tosh. We hadn't seen each other in a week.

"What happened?"

"I don't know, String Bean. You forced Maria to call me. You were crying, yelling that only I would understand. I came over, but, before Maria would leave, she had to make sure that I wouldn't do anything to you. That Maria, she still doesn't trust me. But, yeah, you cried and told me you missed me before passing out."

None of it made sense.

How did I not remember any of this?

It seemed beyond dramatic, so much so that Maria had missed the entirety of our first campus festival all because of my drunk ass.

Tosh and I met Maria at the field.

"Oh, thank god!"

She wrapped me into a hug.

"Dude, what happened?"

"I don't know. What did you drink? You were going berserk. I've never seen you like that before."

"What? I don't know. I had two shots at Theresa's, and then we ate before going to the Genesee house, where Nicole gave me a drink. I don't remember after that. What happened?"

"Well, you were punching people and spitting on them."

"What?!"

"You broke Leena's camera."

"Oh, no."

"You fell down in front of a cop, laughing hysterically, and wouldn't move. I thought they were going to have you arrested, so I took you back to your dorm room where you started fighting me. I tried to get you to drink water, but you knocked it out of my hands."

"That explains the wet spot."

"Then you became impossibly inconsolable, begging for me to call Tosh. So I did. I wrote you the note, so you wouldn't be afraid."

"Thank you. Oh my god. Maria, I am so sorry."

"Yeah. It was pretty scary."

I replayed the scene that Maria had relayed to me, none of us laughing like we normally would, looking for the last lucid moment before the black hole of memory loss.

When Nicole handed me the red cup that she didn't want.

There was something in that drink.
A drug that makes you forget everything and lose all control of your bodily responses.
A violation of my rights by someone who had initially planned to roofie Nicole but had spiked me instead.

O riginally a byproduct, these social features had eclipsed the main reason we went to higher educational institutions in the first place.

I was one of many learning on an assembly-line system of mass certification. Two hundred and fifty bodies were dispersed throughout a concrete auditorium where sound struggled to reach the last couple rows of students in the back, which were ironically the first rows to be occupied. I was one of many asked to sit still for fifty minutes, spending the excess time between copying sentences from each new slide hiding behind a screen of web pages and chatting with friends on Facebook. I was one of many practicing this disrespectful dance of diverting my attention for a grand total of ten hours across Mondays, Wednesdays, and Fridays. I was one of many who misrepresented studying by calling what I did—its opposite—my rai·son d'ê·tre. Because I was one of many glorified adolescents roaming an interconnected system of sterile lecture halls, pungent dining halls, overpopulated libraries, and secondhand dorms with too much time on my hands and too little guidance. I was one of many who did not consider what the government or my parents subsidizing all this time for me to learn meant because I was one of many internalizing all that this new environment was subtly telling me without any constructive outlet available to process it. I was one of many contemplating suicide or drinking because I did not feel connected to anyone or anything, taking Adderall or championing all-nighters because I only spent one night a week actually studying. I was one of many not asking myself why I was there—because I already knew the answer.

It's what I'm supposed to do.

I considered partying to be my first exercise of freedom. I thought I was reclaiming my power when I was actually rebelling against eighteen years of someone else controlling how I led my life.

I had removed all boundaries to see what it meant to let everything forbidden in. None of the consequences—black-out hangovers, confusion over how my body works, two rounds of pink eye and four rounds of strep throat, getting roofied—held an associated judgment because no one around me abided by consequences either.

My role models weren't my parents or my teachers.

My role models were people I had just met who happened to be experts in the "dangerous things" I had never been allowed to do. To be worthy of an invitation to hang with them, I had to present myself as indifferent to consequences. When, in practice, it wasn't indifference as much as it was disregard.

Sophomore Year

Although debauchery painted the larger strokes of freshman year, there were still fibers of responsibility providing my life's form with stability. I nannied for two children, held a leadership role in my sorority, and possessed enough forethought to prepare myself for the everlasting light of summer without anyone prompting me to do so.

Two months before summer vacation, I contacted one of the many luxury hotels in Orange County to inquire about seasonal opportunities, and, one painless interview later, I was their towel girl.

On the most basic level, my role consisted of cleaning and organizing, but it quickly became clear that no one was catering to the aquatic center in the same way other departments were known for meeting a guest's needs. I had one co-worker and rarely saw a manager, so it wasn't long before I tapped into the ripe and unclaimed potential of the pool. I began memorizing guests' names, and reserving their preferred chairs without being asked. Depending on the situation, I would even take it one step further, taking note of which paper was their favorite and leaving it for them as well. I was observant, and they liked that. They liked it so much that they handed me twenty-dollar bills for making their days easier.

Aside from these brief spurts of effort, I was getting paid by my direct employer to stare at the ocean, where my mind floated for hours at a time. Having confirmed there was no one to compromise the safety of this open water, thoughts spontaneously drifted to the surface, taking turns tinkering with what it means to think.

I began to consider studying abroad.

By virtue of working for an international company, I was exposed to a range of people, some of whom were visiting from New York for a weekend conference, some from London for a month-long stay, and, most memorably, an eighty-year-old couple who had vacationed at this specific property for the last twenty years. It was the first time I could identify my glaring lack of common ground with the majority of the outside world, whether it was a staff member who used to drive semi-trucks for thirty-six hours straight before earning a more comfortable position as a maintenance employee or an unassuming Holocaust survivor, bundled in his robe, walking through the property holding hands with his wife.

Even though many of my college friends were bilingual, and about half of them had immigrant parents, I had no real precedent for the interactions of this job. The people I partied with weren't mirrors, humbly reflecting my stunted parts back to myself, catalyzing the realization of my lack of cultural intelligence. They were all searching for the same thing as me—an identity—by the most fashionable means possible—getting drunk.

One afternoon, I happened to meet the radio announcer for the San Diego Padres while working at the towel distribution area.

He was wearing a Padres baseball cap, so I mentioned that I went to school at UCSD.

"Very nice. What are you studying?"

"Communications."

He nodded, reaching into his pocket.

"Here."

It was his business card.

"Let me know if you're ever looking for an internship."

He casually took the towels he had originally come for and walked away.

I did not possess a hidden agenda of advancing myself, talking to every guest I met, looking to rub elbows with a VIP. I just wanted to establish common ground. And, through this extension of my genuine interest in others, my wandering thoughts had been confirmed.

Multiple limbs grew from the trunk of my degree in communications, all with an appeal more stimulating than that of the precarious branch of sorority life I had dangled from freshman year. The leaves supported by my future were crisp with the untapped potential of travel, vibrant with opportunity, and representative of my courage to extend myself outside what was comfortable.

I had a reason to start growing up.

It was fall quarter, which meant sorority recruitment. **AKA: Rush.**

Each potential candidate entered the room overwhelmed by the hundred sets of eyes lunging at her, hypnotizing her with a never-ending chain of forced smiles, all the while serenading her to a song we had finished memorizing the lyrics to the night before.

Out of nowhere, an existing member would link into her arm, still singing, and guide her to an assigned spot within the decorated three-hundred-square-foot conference room. This was a logical next step in her mind; the rest of the girls rushing needed to squeeze into the remaining space before the piercing roar of two hundred women speaking all at once began. Although distinctly out of her element, she was captivated. The cohesion of our group was endearing, if not romantic.

25

But, little did she know, every move had been orchestrated. One existing member had volunteered to organize the sacrament of recruitment, taking on the responsibility of knowing as much as she can about every girl applying for sisterhood; information that a specifically arranged group of members—who were assigned to talk to her—extracted during the first day of recruitment. From there, the rush administrator arranged an even more nuanced pairing process to increase the chances of this girl choosing us by placing her with girls similar to herself throughout the next four days. She is surprised by how comfortable she feels, an uncanny kinship to girls she's just happening to meet, if not supposed to meet, because it's fate, right?

The methodology behind the practice was exposing how much I had changed over the summer.

We gave presentations to the potential members regarding our philanthropy events, intramural sports, and leadership roles, when, in reality, none of us were concerned with the technicalities of it all.

Some of us were shopping for an identity while the rest of us were strutting down the catwalk, intentionally unaware of the mold of perfection we were falsely advertising.

During the first month of school, I had returned to nannying, but it wasn't sufficient supplemental funding like it had been a year ago. Subletting my big sis's room while she studied abroad in Greece made the cost of living and dining readily apparent. I was watching my towel girl savings disintegrate, anticipating dinner with my parents the coming week when I would address the unprecedented situation.

Over the entrée, I sharply turned into the topic, "I noticed that you guys haven't put any money in my account this year," before slamming into a bite of food.

There wasn't gleeful reception or even surprise. There was only, "We can't do that anymore."

Loaded brevity fell like a bomb silently detonating on the ocean floor. I looked away to avoid asking what it had meant. I tried not to ask what things meant because my mom always asked me too many questions about everything. So, instead, I internalized her statement, obsessing for the next couple weeks over what to do next.

I stopped going out on Fridays despite the endless invitations from Tosh and other friends because, for the first time ever, I wanted to be alone. I wanted to see the conditions of myself and how those integral parts of my being applied to the larger, outer play of life.

What did being nineteen mean?
What role did my family play in my life?

I had just spent my freshman year rejecting how I had been raised. Yet I could feel the invisible tug of obligation by the expression that usurped my mother's face at dinner, suggesting an inner battle I had never detected before.

Throughout this lifelong development process, layers of the veil— through which we make sense of the world—will be shed.

It is not provoked but cyclical; we cannot force it to happen. It just happens.

For instance, on one ordinary high school day, I made the connection that material goods hold another value beyond monetary price. They can also serve as signifiers, defining who a person is and the lifestyle they lead. But it wasn't until my mother's suggestion that we did not belong to this group of privilege that it rooted deeper into my mind.

Up until then, I had always regarded survival as an archaic form of existence, recreated on the reality show, *Survivor.* But as I began to flip through memories, I could recall many subtle moments between my parents and their adult counterparts, at pre-homecoming parties and the like, that were short lived, if they even happened at all. I had presumed that most divisions between people were predicated on either a disagreement or incompatibility, never before considering that these nuances could be due to an invisible cord of tension determined by class. Or, on an even more sophisticated level, that my parents projected their own judgments of themselves onto other adults whose lives they assumed were easier because they had more money.

Although we didn't own expensive cars, live in a mansion, or tote Louis Vuitton, I would have never labeled my parents as victims of struggle, doing what they could to make ends meet.

We were just different.

The next Monday in class, a girl in my sorority asked me if I had gone out that past weekend.

"No."

I redirected my attention to my notebook.

I did not need to explain to her that I was reconciling the shadow of freshman year, the widow of the person who I once portrayed myself to be.

"Oh, well I saw Tosh leave the Delta house with Jackie Williams on Saturday morning."

"Excuse me?"

This girl—my "sister"—and I rarely spoke, yet she knew she had vital information that I needed to hear.

"Yeah. He was with Jessica Hernandez all night on Friday at the Sigma party, too."

The taste of bile swarmed my mouth, fumes from the pit in my stomach enveloped my vital organs, heart, and soul.

Just then, Tosh texted me.

Tosh: *Let's get lunch when you're out?*

Me: *Of course.*

His decision to hook up with two girls was not a literal breach of our relationship since I was no longer technically his girlfriend. But the part I failed to mention above was that he had invited me to go out that past Friday when I told him I didn't feel well. I didn't think anything of his unannounced drop in the next morning to take me to my favorite breakfast spot beyond his thoughtfulness. He listened while I incoherently cried through my confusion over all that my mother hadn't said and what I should do. Reassuring myself by telling myself that he was my best friend, my vulnerability gave way to us having sex back at my place. Depleted of energy by the time we finished, I told him to go along to Saturday's party without me.

So, no, his decision to potentially sleep with two strange girls— girls with names I had never heard before—that same weekend was not a breach of a romantic relationship. It was how I learned what the word **violation** meant.

I waited for him in the food court, pretending to eat my lunch as he sprung in, unassuming, placing a kiss on my cheek.

He playfully sat beside me, but no matter how convincing his sweetness was, I would not surrender my nerve.

"I know what you did this weekend."

"What do you mean, Bean?"

His gentle voice of feigned ignorance was enough confirmation for me.

"I don't want to talk to you ever again."

I dramatically abandoned the food I had no appetite for anyway, forging a path through the lunchtime crowd.

"I don't know what you're talking about."

He followed me as I wove through students going about their own business. I could feel him catching up when I stopped, turning to look him straight in the eye.

"Go. **Away**."

Suspended by my words, motionless by the prick of my tone, he remained as I faded into the distance.

A virtue of humanity instilled in me by my parents—one of the few that'd stuck—was that relationships are built on trust, forming a see-saw between the hearts of two people.

This balance beam is extremely sensitive, influenced by even the slightest shift in one of the two individuals, both of whom are constantly shifting their individual wants, needs, thoughts, and feelings as they move throughout their day. Without verbalization of said moments, the see-saw quickly falls out of balance, bruising tailbones and breeding resentment. Initially, we might laugh at the sudden plummet into unforgivable sand, justifying it with whatever comes to mind. But, if that pattern continues to repeat itself, and we avoid reestablishing equilibrium through open communication, then the giant welts on our tailbones will throb until we finally admit that something isn't right.

Many relationships will end, and such dissolution cannot be avoided because these former partners (and/or friends) are preparing us for what is to come.

Therefore, **failure** (AKA: an endeavor not turning out the way we wanted it to) is a necessary part of learning because it provides us with information. We are often quick to construe it as negative because it hurts, and we cannot understand why all that was no longer is. So we avoid our confusion, covering it up with denial and justifications, imposing our will upon the natural forces of change. But the universe will not stop sending us the same lesson until we acknowledge the aspects of our lives that are demanding our attention.

These perceived failures are actually gateways to self-awareness that not only impact the way we see the world but who we choose to surround ourselves with.

Tosh's decision facilitated my own. It was the impulsive kind. The kind when our gut pushes our mind out of the way because the gut has things it wants us to do that the mind cannot yet comprehend.

I called my dad.

"I'm moving home."

"If that's what you want to do."

His voice trailed off.

He wasn't telling me not to do it, but he wasn't telling me to do it either. The second major decision of my early adult life.

"I'm going to call the hotel to see if they have any open positions, and I'll go to UCI next quarter to make the transition easier."

"Okay. Love you."

"Love you, too."

During the month and a half I had left living in San Diego, I became inseparable from my roommate, Jess.

She had just broken up with her boyfriend as well, so we fell back onto one another, assuming the other's void as our own. She introduced me to yoga—a refuge that would be invaluable to my future—and we practiced religiously before our casual Wednesday and Thursday night hang outs. Jess and I would split a fifth of vodka with two other friends before passing out around two a.m., only to arouse a mere six hours later to show my miserable face during a nine a.m. section before doing it all over again.

The annual ugly sweater party, commemorating the end of fall quarter, had arrived.

I would begin my new position as a front desk agent at the hotel I had worked at over the summer the following week. A transition delineated by imaginary dotted lines, separating this understood part of my life from the ambiguous next step into the unknown. Jess and I had gotten ready and gone to the party with different friend groups, and there was a blank space between my arrival and waking up the next morning on a couch I had never seen before.

I had severe pounding in my head, disorientation, and bodily exhaustion. It was possible that I had been tossed out of a moving garbage truck as part of a new drinking game. Luckily, tradition upheld, and there was a handwritten note waiting atop the coffee table.

Hey Cee!

Hope you are feeling better. We took you back from the A D Pi party last night. Let us know if you need anything!

Signed, Eleanor

Who the fuck was Eleanor?

I mean, Eleanor could be considered one of the most memorable names ever. Why couldn't I place this person?

Oh yeah, it's because I internally doused myself in alcohol to the point that I was impressed with my retained ability of translating strings of letters into coherent sentences if not the capacity to note that I was not wearing shoes nor was I in possession of my keys or phone.

My S.O.S. call would have to wait until this Eleanor character, a potential prophet of god, manifested from her dwelling and revealed herself unto me. And, with that, I fell back asleep.

I naturally awoke to the sound of subdued commotion. A stranger was standing in the frame of the outlet that separated the living room from the bedrooms.

"Hey," she sympathetically sung.

"Eleanor?"

"No. I'm Samantha."

Someone else peeked her head out from behind the wall.

"Hey, Cee!"

Oh. My. God.

It was a girl from one of my writing class sections.

Eleanor.

We had never hung out outside of section, and she had maybe proofread a paper of mine once.

"Hey," I moaned less enthusiastically and, without trying to sound like I do this all the time, asked, "So what happened last night?"

Samantha and Eleanor shared a look, as if they had pulled straws to determine who would be the unlucky bearer of news.

"Well, we went to the ugly sweater party," Samantha started.

Eleanor chimed in, "And I drove."

"And we had to park really far away. It was dark, and we didn't know how to get out of the neighborhood."

"We were driving down this random street when we saw a person—you—lying on the front yard of someone's house."

I covered my mouth with my hand.

Eleanor nodded. "So, I was like, *Oh my god! That's Cee from MMW.* We stopped just as you woke up, brushing yourself off, not noticing us, before taking off down the street."

"So we stopped you and asked you where you were going. You said, *Home,* and kept walking. We stopped you again to ask where that was, and you said, *Muir.*"

"We brought you back here to campus because you didn't have any of your stuff and couldn't tell us where you lived."

They waited for my response.

I was suppressing tears at their confirmation of the utter disarray that was my life.

> *How could I have gotten so out of control as to be streets away from the original house?*

Better yet:

> *How could I be fortunate enough to have this girl—an unaffiliated classmate—find me?*

Withholding sorority girl sobs, I genuinely gave them an *I'm sorry* and *Thank you so much* capped with a *Do you have a computer I can borrow?*

Eleanor casually filled the gap of silence after handing me her laptop.

"So what apartments do you live in?"

"Oh, I don't live on campus."

"That's weird that you said that you lived in Muir then."

I just smiled.

I logged into Facebook, searching friends online for anyone who was more credible than me, striking gold. My grand big, Beverly, was not only online but was more than willing to help.

Beverly: *I'll be there as soon as I can.*

As I climbed into the safety of her car, the clogged worry, disappointment in myself, and near-death level of irresponsibility faded away. Her authentic Beverly smile reached out, reassuring me that none of this was as bad as it seemed. She would drive us to the house the party had been at, where we would get it all sorted out.

We arrived during the dawn of a hangover.

The door slid inward at Lurch's pace. T-Bev—one of the fraternity brothers who lived in the house that threw the party—warily crept from behind the edge of the door.

"Thank god. It's not the cops!" he yelled back into the house behind him before widening the door to its fullest extent. "Cee!"

"T-Bev! What happened last night? Do you have my stuff?"

"Dude, you disappeared!"

"No shit. Wait—how do you know that?"

"Because I was with you. You asked me if you could sleep, so I put you in my bed. But then the cops came, and they said that if you didn't wake up they would have to take you to the hospital, so I kept shaking you to wake up. When you did, you sat up and walked out the room liked nothing happened."

"Why didn't you stop me?"

"Dude, I didn't want you to go to the hospital!"

I couldn't deal with his inability to help me right now. I needed to stop expecting other people to help me when I couldn't even help myself.

I ran downstairs to his room.

Everything was there.

I immediately looked at the screen of my phone.

No missed calls, no unanswered texts.

Without Tosh and, I supposed, without Jess, I was on my own team; the resounding note that made leaving the college world behind less painful than if I would have actually had people who cared about me during a time when I felt I needed people most.

I moved myself back home, unloading my furniture into the office downstairs since my little brother had acquired my room during the condensed four months of my sophomore year.

My new living quarters was comparable to the size of a shed, unable to contain all of my things; the irony of how I had come to regard my life.

I was squeezing back into a container that no longer fit me... Or, was I?

What did it mean to move back home given the unique circumstances? To be back under my parents' roof after having roamed the night as Cee Hunt, a girl who had most recently collapsed onto a stranger's front lawn, readily forgotten by everyone she thought she could trust?

I could not bridge this gap between the person who I was—unfulfilled party animal—and the person who I had no choice but to become—an adult. There were too many moving parts, shifting, rearranging, both internally and externally, and it would have been a lot easier if all I had to do was fall asleep and wake up when it was over.

Moving Home

I ran my hands across my new uniform.

A stiff, white oxford shirt tucked into black boat pants that swallowed my legs. An earbud plugged into a walkie-talkie that was clipped to my waistband. Flat ballerina slippers—which were later deemed inappropriate because socks had been selectively left out as the one defiant act against being told what to do—failed to support an average of nine hours of standing. And my hair was haphazardly compiled atop my head in a ponytail.

I looked as unprepared as I felt.

A rich walnut counter separated the guests from the agents, and a thick wall with two solid wood doors separated the agents from the back of the house. Each front desk employee sported an earpiece that was tuned into the same channel, so managers and valet personnel could communicate with agents for a myriad of reasons.

For instance, if the front of the house was well staffed, during the small window of time it takes to walk into the lobby, the valet would whisper a physical description of the approaching guest with their name through the walkie-talkie so that by the time they arrived at the front desk, we were prepared to impress them by already knowing it. (That one was a show stopper.)

The managers also used it to discuss guest interactions with an agent in real time. So not only would one of us be attempting to solve a problem while faced with a guest's irate and condescending performance, but a manager would chime into our ears making suggestions for how to eradicate the situation more effectively.

How would the managers know what was happening?

There was a live video broadcast onto a small TV in their glorified cave in the back, emitting the only available light other than that of their computer screens.

During my seemingly endless month of training, being lowest on the totem pole, I was treated as such.

The agent training me, Steve, was male, and the other two agents were female. One of them did not regard me as her coworker. I was not even sure that she knew my name since she just looked through me if she ever did glance in my direction.

Steve was an exemplary model of hotel etiquette, eventually accepting a promotion for a managerial position directly from the entry-level role of agent. It was rare that he permitted my completion of any task without his supervision, which is why he had been deemed responsible for my training.

He was meticulous.

A perfectionist.

AKA: he was afraid of failure.

Steve's first act of belief in me was unexpected, though it was born of necessity.

He had to take a bathroom break.

He walked into the back before second-guessing himself, returning to the front again, then finally leaving me to put the registration cards in alphabetical order.

The winds of lost confidence gained strength in his wake, grazing my psyche. I was alphabetizing like I've never alphabetized before until, *"Cee,"* floated into my ear over the crackly lines of the walkie-talkie, thwarting the amplitude of my imagination, *"Can you please come to the back?"*

I wasn't quite sure what my presence was for until I saw my manager from the prior summer standing there. I was cheerful and upbeat at this unforeseen chance at pride, demonstrating to my current managers the rapport I had with managers in other departments.

However, that would not be the case.

She looked at me with the type of expression you would give the one rogue (I would defend them as *adventurous*) preschooler who had not followed the specific directions and had eaten the glue anyway. She made that horrible sound of wet disdain as her tongue hit the back of her teeth. She approached me for what I imagined to be a hug, but her arms went around and above my shoulders. I could feel the tug of her physically dislodging my ponytail like I was a pageant child.

"Um…"

"Oh honey. No, no, no. What do you think we are? The Marriott?"

I was imagining myself screaming at shrill levels like the child I was before kicking her in the shin and running away.

Why was everyone directing their hostility toward me?

Had they not known what I was sacrificing to be here?

Could they not see that I was doing my best?

"Why don't you go down to the bathroom and fix your hair?"

I pivoted to look over my shoulder at my current managers, who were just as flabbergasted by the sheer gall of this lady to touch me without any reasonable cause. My head manager gave me a nod to go ahead, and, with my poofy Gene Wilder hair, I began my walk of shame through the hotel to the employee locker room.

No one else was in there as I stood facing the generic mirror, watching my reflection swallow the lump of humiliation in my throat as teardrops streamed onto the water-stained countertop.

It was clear that my feelings did not matter here.

It did not matter how in over my head I was with the adaptation required to the front desk's innumerable rules and expectations. It did not matter that no one was making the new girl feel comfortable, seeing if there was anything she needed. This establishment was not appealing to me as an individual with unique ideas, sensitivities, and quirks. Rather, sacrificing my individuality was a part of the job description.

I was finally looking at myself.

After four months of trying to make sense of what to do next—avoiding it with late nights of drinking until I passed out—I could no longer prevent where I was going because I was already there.

Looking at myself in the eyes stung. My reflection no longer held the confident vibrance that I had once displayed to the world.

The girl that bounced back from a sudden injury without ever letting on that it had left a formidable wound on her soul. The girl that casually dated Tosh and showed up to parties, singing every word to every rap song in between flip cup and popping from one stale conversation to another. The girl that would pass out on the lawn just to dust herself off and keep going.

All this desperation to be someone had finally caught up to me. I didn't recognize the person staring back at me.

It was official.

I didn't know who I was.

I worked eight- to ten-hour days during the worst shift besides the graveyard shift, three p.m. to eleven-thirty p.m., tumbling into bed at twelve-thirty in the morning, exhausted from the subliminal pressure mixed with my internalization of said pressure.

The all-seeing eye of management was a palpable weight hanging over everyone's heads. Upper administration had brainwashed the department heads into spies, disguising their dirty work as power, belittling and alienating the lemmings like me to either the point of surrender or escape. An unexpected leak of intel from one of Steve's subconscious gaskets confirmed all this my fourth week there.

Supposedly there was a high turnover of agents at the front desk (which is probably why they had no choice but to hire me) because it was difficult to retain employees who not only wanted to work there but could handle the responsibility and stress of the job. The latest horror story he divulged was about one of the most recent managers—a recipient of numerous company awards—who had been terminated because his cashier's bank count was off by two dollars. A two-thousand-dollar bank that each front desk agent, including myself, was responsible for.

After three months of attending UCI, I transferred back to UCSD, driving down there on my days off for class.

By then, I was working earlier shifts at the front desk, yet my newfound time was not a source of relief because, now, it coincided with that of my parents'.

Not only could I see how the current financial situation was affecting them, but I could feel its second-hand poison infiltrating my body.

My mother was harsh while my father complained.

My father had been a real estate agent during the economic collapse, and, since nobody dared dip their hands in that sullied sector of industry, he had resigned himself to working at a retail store, regarding his temporary job as beneath him. He lamented the long hours of standing on his feet amidst the lack of organization and coherence of his fellow employees while my mother rolled her eyes at his disapproval.

From the moment she came home from yet another twelve-hour work day of teaching and tutoring Cog Sci at the community college, she streamed through the house like a stealth submarine. We all stayed out of her way, never prompting too much, because we never knew if she was aggravated by stress and attack-mode ready, or if she was just exhausted and didn't want to talk. Meanwhile, my younger brother would clandestinely remove himself into his teenage dungeon of a room. He was an eighth grader, hiding from the inevitable pain of a world larger than himself. A realm he could see but had yet to be summoned to.

While I was being tossed around like a cracked egg, whipped by ambient pain, scrambled into a life I had never seen for myself, much less could understand.

The vessel of my body had been seized by a pathogenic case of asphyxiating anxiety, extinguishing my normally ravenous appetite and fogging my once lucid mind. My drive home would be colored by instant replays of moments from work that day. I would analyze each action I took that could have been interpreted as a punishable offense, turning these self-proposed, realistically indeterminable mistakes and their subsequent consequences into my likely reality. My surmounting angst during the twelve hours between my last and my next shift was as all the evidence I needed to confirm that life as I knew it was on the edge of collapse once again.

My entrapment in a malfunctioning body and enslavement to the irrationality of a fractured mind were both symptoms of my ego's pursuit of control over a world that it had just learned functioned on the unknown. The unknown wasn't the freedom to party that quasi-connected me to others who did the same. The unknown was a plunge into darkness so disorienting—thus, inexplicable—that I felt alienated from everyone I knew.

I had yet to realize that there are limits to our empathy, the corruption of which are expectations. I assumed out of all people to understand the difficulty of what it meant to move back home it would be my friends from high school. But how could they? Things were unwavering for them—friend groups, parties, athletics, and economic stability—which is why they couldn't empathize. I represented the worst that could happen; a situation many of them would never have to imagine much less live through.

In order to avoid feeling hurt by the lack of people there asking

me if everything was okay, I kept telling myself that I could handle
all of this on my own until crying myself to sleep night after night
seemed toilsome for the sake of anonymous martyrdom. My will
was not strong enough to vanquish the suffocation of loneliness
without a support system, encouraging me to grow closer to the last
person I would have ever expected to.

My mom.

My inability to cope was an extension of hers. We would meet
for dinner after our extended work days, our conversations
haphazardly supporting our newfound relationship. We fed one
another's biased complexes regarding the nonexistence of money,
the incompetence of my father, the trials of jobs that don't make
us happy, and all the other people who suck because they don't
understand, they don't care, or both.

B y summer, my vulnerability had calloused, challenging my stress
and anxiety to develop a more clever way of getting through.

I lost twenty pounds and was diagnosed with IBS, leading
a chronically bloated existence, spontaneously developing a
sensitivity to many of the foods I was accustomed to eating. I did
not feel physically well on most days, transforming eating from a
ritual I reveled in into a precarious necessity. But no one at home
designated this as a side-effect of my free fall into the unknown
because no one could see me in general.

The institutions I had been trained to abide by—school and
sports—rewarded students who fulfilled what is expected of them
with grades, praise, and the self-satisfaction of being objectively
correct. But, so far, the adult world had taught me that fulfilling
what was expected of me wasn't as much of an accomplishment as
it was the standard of being employed. This was the first of many
conclusions I would draw from this disparate world of color, but
before close examining the details of any other stroke, I needed to
grasp the context of the picture at large.

Like how we will spend twenty-two years going through the
monochrome motions in preparation for the adult world of

pigments and hues, shadows and texture, but that it only takes days between graduation and *what now?* for our guts to feel heavy from realizing the difference between theory and practice. We soothe the degree we still owe money on with our collegiate validation until enough tangles with the textbook print we paid to memorize and this spiraling wheel of color crawls from our guts into our hearts stirring them awake. Tension and anxiety begin to take root. We are secretly waiting for someone else to confirm the same within themselves, but all most longtime-color residents want to know is if we have a job yet. So we bypass this glaring illusion by continuing to follow our elders' coaxing. Without addressing our disappointment over four years of investing in a degree that doesn't matter, we continue climbing up the social ladder, lubricating our bruised hearts and our queasy guts with the renewed confidence that this next rung will bring us the satisfaction that the previous accomplishment could not. That a well-compensated position at a cutting-edge company with stock options that will pay out big once they sell are the promise to that studded future the degree had not guaranteed.

We favor their advice over our intuitive hesitation because their inability to feel what we feel is our norm. That is why they had not confirmed the discrepancy within our hearts as valid, and that is why we didn't question the disparity. It never occurred to us to inspect further into the *why* behind these palpable, yet unspoken, differences.

On a subconscious level, we know of the private memories that they ardently avoid without fully making the connection that these memories of their origin stories are the same reason why we don't discuss the moments that make our own hearts itch. That their hidden truths are the reason why they've never been able to feel what we feel, and why life looks differently to them. That life is a linear trajectory of putting your head down until you get to where you want to be because the mechanism in their hearts that locates the seismic waves of their path stopped performing regular maintenance long ago.

As children, many of them spent years tiptoeing through the

minefield of a toxic household. They didn't grow up to extract the shards from the shattering of their illusions to assess them because they were just happy that it wasn't literal shrapnel. Nor did they try to change the system because life wasn't about bringing justice to the professional world as much as it was feeling safe in a world plagued by traumatic childhoods, war, riots, racism, gender inequality, and stagflation. (Sound familiar?) When, as in any generation, there was a divergence amongst them. There were some who wandered—who were hippies, who became artists, or who got arrested—while others got the jobs that saved them— eventually coaching us to take the same well-traveled path—and the rest—who also expected to redeem their stunted youth by becoming a prominent someone—were granted the unexpected onset of parenthood instead. For the employed group, their career status became the source of their pride and their immunity to the pain of the confusion of life. And, for the parents lacking financial security, their children became the source of their redemption and the perpetuation of their self-sacrifice. The former played golf, went to dinner with family friends, and didn't worry about anything that did not directly endanger their external comforts. While the latter told us to keep dreaming and to keep striving because we were special, deserving, and worthy so that once we were old enough, we wouldn't be slighted like they had been. They raised us with the love they hadn't received, strengthening our sensitivity, shielding us from danger and strife within an illusory world built by their doing anything to make odds and ends meet when all we had ever wanted was someone to say all of this. To be forthcoming with the *why* instead of guarded with the **what**.

Without class, I had more time to pick at these spontaneous connections when my nail pushed through a gap in the matrix.

My mother's censorship when sharing details of my parents' financial instability, fueling her relentless dismissal of my father as an equal partner, was virtually nonexistent. She was spewing the precise facts she had fervidly concealed from me up until a year ago, negating herself without awareness of this contradiction.

Where was my mom?

Where had the woman obsessed with protecting me from the ugly head of the other side of life gone?

She was finally communicating the honesty I had waited nineteen years to receive, but all I could hear was anger from people who had once made themselves out to be the guardians to the gates of reality. Even though they were obviously robed in the orange jumpsuits of prisoners, I had trusted their word above everything else.

So I just sat there, silently nodding along with what she said as the definitive knowing that I would be moving back to San Diego for my junior year solidified in my head. I needed geographical separation to not only regain sanity and perspective but to seize what was left of my youth because the revelation of truth was disillusioning to the point of denial.

When the scene of what we've always considered constant and true cracks, it does not always obfuscate our ability to see because the scene is our norm, our failsafe, our only perspective. Therefore, to us, the truth is what the cracks are separating, not the cracks themselves. It is too overwhelming to think that the whole of our lives and what we thought about the people closest to us was a lie. It doesn't make sense. We would have to review the entirety of our past, searching for clues to prove the preposterous suggestion that we spent however many years refining our understanding of the world just to be shown that the ground upon which we stand is not concrete. So we distract ourselves with the immediate demands of the present until the cracks dip into valleys and our stability is eradicated by a catastrophic natural disaster that involuntarily wipes the slate clean.

Back to School

I no longer saw the point.

Going to class just to chase the monotonous boredom away with barely memorable taco Tuesdays and sushi nights?

My reintroduction to my peers during sorority recruitment made me realize how little they knew, reinforcing that same piece of disconnect that had isolated me from others while living at home.

Real life teetered on high stakes, and college was just a sleight of hand distracting us from these practical facts.

Greek life allowed us to insulate ourselves within a world of tomfoolery that some elders repeatedly recalled *the best years of our lives*. We did not notice the redundancies in our education or question the inconsistencies because we just wanted to enjoy life. We did not challenge a professor's opinion presented as truth, but, rather, we worshiped what they said out of projected ignorance.

> *They obviously know more about life than us, that's why they are professors.*

This hierarchy pacified our minds because we knew our place. Our ability to think was determined by the coherence of a written argument in which we repeated what other people thought about gender and race. Our worldviews were justified by academia, based upon hegemonic theory, thus lessening the chance of a revolution.

Because our education put us on a pedestal. We would never accuse the system that led us to our achievements of being a false reality based on controlling how we think and act via textbook manipulation.

College was liberating and progressive, not an extension of our educational incarceration.

S ubject material never addressed the issue of modern-day survival. That's what the financial aid office was for. But I didn't see that student loan money because my parents used it to offset the burden.

So it was up to me.

It was up to me to both take care of myself and reconcile the things I had seen. The last year of my life outside these illusory walls that claimed to nurture and empower had awakened an unknown part of myself. Something undefinable that I would temporarily label *pride*.

This chip on my shoulder masked my vulnerability and craved a new challenge. I already knew I could go to school while working a full-time job and still get A's. I needed something I had never done before. Something that would bring justice to this broken world.

I needed to help others.

O ne week and one interview later, I was the events intern for a nonprofit organization.

Despite my glaring lack of experience, my eager first impression must have come off as confident because by the two-month mark, the CEO made an unexpected announcement. She was moving back to Chicago after having only spent three months in their new satellite office here.

Of course, anyone's gears would turn with selfish curiosity, but the CEO was quick to reassure.

"We are shutting down the office here, yes. But, that doesn't mean anything's going to change. The fundraiser is still happening. It just means that you are going to be in charge of everything from now on."

She meant that I would go from writing grant proposals and marketing material to recruiting sponsors and negotiating permits with the city. She meant that I would go from about six hours of work in the office to about twelve hours of work outside of my hostessing job and twenty units of classwork.

And, just like that, I had returned to the comfort of chaos.

I was filling the wounded space inside myself with more than I could handle to justify my placement in a world that didn't make sense, sharpening the chip on my shoulder with my self-inflicted victimization. I was cordial but distant with everyone except a classmate I met during rush whose pointed spikes also preemptively shielded a gooey heart.

Regina and I sitting in the food court at Whole Foods, discussing esoteric ideas and our peers' ignorance of the real world was more magnetizing than anything I had experienced up to that point. Life had slapped her across the face a few times, and we stirred one another's juvenile cynicism, reinforcing one another's obscure intellects, forming my first ever synergetic relationship.

Since neither of us enjoyed frat parties, it was uncharacteristic for us to do anything "fun" outside of ordering both wine and dessert at dinner. But when Regina's boyfriend couldn't make the Timbaland benefit concert he had gotten them tickets to, as best friend, I naturally assumed the role of escort.

And I.

Was.

PUMPED.

I didn't even care that she declared I would be driving the three-hour, traffic-induced trip because she had to cram for a mid-term.

I *fucking* loved Timbaland.

The tickets were waiting with a courier at the Peninsula Hotel in Beverly Hills. We rolled into the pristine aura of the lobby, distinctly out of place among the refined edges of wealth, swiftly scoping out the closest powder room where we could freshen up. I shimmied into a Forever 21 romper while Regina sported a tube top and high-waisted jeans. Failing to compensate for our youth with our costume change—but, rather, aiming to glorify it—we cruised back through the lobby and into the bar to be greeted by young (older than us) professionals who were probably drinking scotch on the rocks (whatever that tasted like) and wanted to buy us drinks. Although we were both twenty and appreciated the offer, we had only stopped by to pick up our tickets from them, reassuring their bruised egos that we would catch up with them later at the concert.

We approached the concierge desk with the portrayed confidence of a hotel guest to ask the employee for a nearby restaurant recommendation. He informed us that sushi would be the closest and easiest. We drove the two minutes across the street, easily pulling into an available parking space in the unassuming concrete strip mall.

We entered the cozy establishment, opting for seats next to the only two patrons there. Regina and I performed the designated roles of our friendship. She chose the food while I took in the surroundings. I audibly gasped and turned to shake Regina.

"Oh my god! Regina, do you know who is sitting next to us?" I said in what was intended to be a restrained whisper.

She looked over my shoulder and sat back in my line of view, unfazed.

"No. And, I really need to keep studying."

"Regina what is wrong with you?"

I was not whispering. I realized it, and reeled it in.

"It's Tony Bennett!"

"Who's Tony Bennett?"

For someone who could recite Voltaire from memory, I shouldn't have been shocked by her lack of pop culture knowledge.

"Never mind."

I was on the verge of peeing my pants from the pings of electricity by being this close to a living legend.

I interrupted her again.

"I'm going to ask him for a picture."

"Go for it," she said without bothering to look up from her notecards.

I was vibrating. My mouth was dry. I would not talk myself out of a moment like this.

With a gap of a mere foot between us, there was an anticlimactic amount of room to cover. I tapped him on the shoulder as politely as a stranger could to a living piece of musical history.

"Excuse me? Mr. Bennett? I am so sorry to interrupt you, but may I bother you for a picture?"

I think he gurgled something unintelligible to himself—along the lines of *Why won't they just leave me alone?*—and there was a long pause before he motioned to me to give the camera to his significant other. I wasn't breathing during the picture—wearing a deer-in-headlights expression—kicking off the trend for the rest of the night.

The following events proceeded at an arm's length distance from the stage where we happened to be sat at Timbaland's VIP table. We met both Cedric the Entertainer and Will-I-Am as well as watched multiple musical performances in a scene resembling that of a backyard pool party all while sipping on mixed drinks made from industrial-sized bottles of Belvedere.

The LA scene was magnetizing.

Ambition threw flames from people's eyes. They were functioning products of a work hard, play hard atmosphere, which I not only appreciated but was determined to be a part of.

We drove back to school before the concert ended, returning at the cusp of dawn. I crawled into bed for a power nap before class, but my heart resisted falling out of this waking dream.

My first encounter with this supernatural place they call LA, and I had already contracted the itch.

The event for my internship was rapidly approaching. My field-study project for my ESL volunteer role required significant attention, and I had not had a break in almost two years. So when Regina suggested that we take advantage of low fares and book tickets to New York for spring break, I knew we had to go.

The day before we left, I called Regina as soon as I had taken my last final to gush over our impending trip.

She was going to drive up to my parents' house later that day, so they could drop us off at the airport early the next morning. But, by nightfall, not only had she not arrived, she had not called me back.

Nope.

She did not call me back until around midnight that night to divulge that she could no longer go to New York.

"I don't understand. What do you mean you can't go?"

Her voice had taken on the tone of a flatline monitor.

"I don't have enough money."

If you knew you didn't have enough money, you would have known this prior to the immediate hours leading up to our departure.

"Okay. Then ask your dad for money."

Silence.

"I can't do that. I just can't go. I'm sorry."

Her sorry fell upon deaf ears.

I had granted Regina the role *witness to my life*, investing my entire portfolio of redemptive energy in her under the assumption that this was a mutual fund. But that it was not. It was not because none of my relationships ever had been. I kept repeating the same dense patterns, assuming that this was finally the person who would understand, who would complete me, just to watch them self-detonate after a few months (or years) of growing close.

51

I crawled into bed with my mom unable to console myself.
That vicious word *hate* sank into my bones. Another round of
disillusionment atrophying the viable marrow that remained.
But all was not lost.
I had made plans to stop in Texas to visit one of my friends from
high school on the leg back from New York. So I adapted to the new
situation by extending my stay with her when it dawned on me.
Gregg also goes to school in Texas.

Who is Gregg?

*Gregg is a boy from my high school whom I reconnected with
at a party over Christmas break.*

AKA: we hooked up, I had dinner at his parents' house
before he returned to school, and he sent me a Build-A-
Bear on Valentine's Day.

Was it confusing?

Absolutely.

But I cared more about my curiosity than I did my
clarity.

"Hey. I'm thinking about making a trip to Texas next week. Would
you like to meet up if you're going to be around?"
"I would love to see you! When are you thinking about coming?"
"When do you have time next week?"
"Come for the weekend. I'll get a hotel room. I may have to be
gone for some fencing practices, but you can use my car in the
interim."
My smile blocked the bleeding.

This boy wanted me to come see him in his element.

This boy was going to make it work with his schedule.

*This boy was not as close to me as Regina, yet was fulfilling a
duty that my best friend could not.*

52

He picked me up in Dallas and was exactly how I remembered him. Warm and calm. He had driven three hours just to come get me before driving three hours back again.

The prince with perfect timing.

A real-life reunion morphed into a fantasy-glazed, romantic comedy through my eyes.

Cartoon butterflies, representing my nervous anticipation, fluttered out my belly button, farting a rainbow of redemption that would slide into a happy ending.

We pulled up to the hotel, darkness at its peak. He checked us into the room we would be sharing, neither of us saying much as we navigated wallpapered halls, leading us to what we both knew came next.

He placed down our bags without switching on the lights, turning to face me, a swift motion that fluidly pressed our bodies against the bed. His decision to forgo awkward foreplay chatter informed me that we were on the same page, having both been deprived of intimate relations since the last time we'd met.

I spent the following day alone. Gregg had practice, so I meandered through the sleepy town until we reconvened at the hotel before dinner that night. But he was not eagerly soaking up my being, offering himself like he once had over Christmas or the night before.

His gaze fell beyond the contour of my face, ignoring the fragile self across from him who was subliminally begging him to fill the waxing wound of her soul.

I received single-word answers to my questions.

Are you hungry? **Sure.**

How was practice? **Fine.**

But I refused to forfeit my chance at happiness.
"Let's play the question game!" I suggested.
"What's that?"
"Well, you think of a question that you want to know about me, and I answer. And then I do the same to you, and we keep going back and forth."
He was indifferent yet submitted anyway.
I sat there for a few loaded moments as he resumed his former disengaged pose.
"Are you gonna ask me something?"
"I thought you were gonna ask me."
"Okay."
So I asked first, but the game only lasted two rounds. He was more concerned with the professional sports featured on the TV screens behind my head.

We actively avoided eye contact while brushing our teeth before getting into bed. He nimbly rolled onto his side to turn out the light without saying *good night.*

Although this would have been an appropriate time to take a hint, my splintered vulnerability had disabled my appropriate response mechanism to social cues.
"What's wrong?"
He grudgingly rolled onto his back, the contour of his stomach reflecting off the glare of the hotel window.
"We can't do this. I already told you I don't want a girlfriend right now. And that's what you want. You want me to be your boyfriend."
Tears silently streamed down my cheeks.
"I don't know what you mean."
"You know when you asked me why I didn't text you back, and I said that we aren't allowed to have our phones in class?"

He was referencing a phone discussion soon after he had returned to school.

"I lied. I can have my phone in class."

That was the last comment he made before turning back onto his side, ending the conversation.

Maybe he was unaware that he had just stabbed my raging sore with a rusty dagger, and maybe he wasn't; but I cried myself to sleep that night, silently choking on the burning ache in my chest. I had never suspected I would be so uncomfortable with him, this impostor who accused me of a claim I had never vocally made.

The next morning, I woke up alone. He had a team meeting, and after replaying the fractured episode to my mother on the phone, I decided it'd be best for me to leave. I waited for him to return, seated on the edge of the cardboard comforter, my suitcase propped vertically against my leg.

"No, please don't go. We can still have fun."

What the fuck?

Why on earth would he want me to stay after what happened last night? I had not forced him to invite me, and his change of heart had me questioning my sanity.

"I don't see how that can happen, Gregg. Just let me go home."

"We're supposed to go back to Dallas tonight. Let's just go and have a good time. It'll be fun."

I caved.

Not because I thought that this time he would certainly fall in love with me, but because I was tired of convincing others to respect my wishes. I dry swallowed the reminder that life is never the way I want it to be before spending the rest of the day shooting glances over my shoulder at the shadow of my disappointment, warning it not to shroud the entirety of my being.

It had been a year and a half now of evading conscious interaction with moments that challenged me to stick up for myself.

I continued to take blows to the face, popping back up like an inflatable doll, inviting the next hit without learning how to dodge or stopping for a wound to congeal. I was bruised and bloody, ignoring the fact that I couldn't see out of my left eye until the swelling in my right eye had compromised my vision altogether.

I returned to school for the last quarter of junior year. The fundraiser happened.

About fifteen people attended, but the CEO could've cared less.

"Cee—this is the best event we have ever done!"

"Uh, really?"

"Yes! This event didn't cost us a dime! You got everything donated: ClifBar, PopChips, Wahoo's, the shirts, the kayaks... Birch Aquarium is here with touch tanks. In the eight years I've been doing this, we've never had something like this!"

She even went as far as potentially offering me a job when I graduated, but the flattery did not register. I could not objectively see what she saw.

Something was missing.

My internal emotional chamber combusted a week later. I called my dad, crying, mumbling incoherent sentences, rambling on for twenty minutes about the tragedy that was my life.

How I had taken on too much. How I couldn't handle it anymore. How the only possible solution was to give up and do something else or go somewhere else completely.

My father listened without interruption before saying the most impactful thing he has ever said to me.

"Whelp, now you know your breaking point. So I guess you won't do that again."

The situation was that simple. *I was the one* making it complicated. I was demanding that situations produce positive outcomes without trying to understand why they weren't first. That is why my life had been so difficult for the past two years. **Life is not a formula.**

There is more involved than just doing what we think we are supposed to do (or what we've been told to do) and tolerating the results regardless of how the reality of those results makes us feel.

I had been inflicting immense pressure upon myself to fit into the social mold of financial security, striving to ensure that I was as viable in the market as possible because I never wanted to put anyone, or myself, in such a consuming position of financial lack—a tide that my parents were still swimming against—again. I kept pushing myself toward tangible goals and accomplishments because all the effort I was investing was bound to make a return. However, my consumption with all of these projects only allowed me to focus on one thing: what I was doing.

I was not asked to be conscious or accountable for the person I depicted myself to be or whether that self was in alignment with who I actually was within. I had not allotted myself the time and attention necessary to tend to all that had happened and how all of it had made me feel because no one had ever taught me how. The only way I knew how to function was through the machinations of my mind; a single processor made solely for calculated solutions. Thus, I had spent two years gathering bitterness from a faulty mode of living.

> *Expecting life to adapt to my pleas regardless of my*
> *willingness to actively engage with what life was showing me*
> *or not showing me.*

I kept waiting for someone or something to acknowledge who I was, all I had been through, and embody the impending miracle that turned my strife around. But that wasn't happening because nobody is responsible for making me happy, fulfilled, or proud.

It was my responsibility to figure out how to do that for myself.

The Five Year Plan

With the scent of greener pastures in LA still lingering in the back of my mind, the idea that I should get an internship there for the summer popped into my head.

But what kind of internship?

What interested me?

The word *film* spewed from the dormant geyser of my subconscious.

Due to its spectacular clarity, I did not deliberate over how I was technically unprepared for it; rather, as quickly as I thought of it, I acted.

Google's algorithm compiled a list of reputable production companies looking for potential interns. I narrowed the companies down, drafted cover letters, and applied, earning two interviews within the same week. The first was in Venice Beach with Michael Bay's Production Company, and the second was via Skype with Ranger Productions, the company responsible for the golden indie teen movie of my adolescence.

I skipped class on a Monday morning to drive the three hours north to Los Angeles, arriving in Venice an hour before my interview with Michael Bay's company.

I scanned the primarily empty street of Abbot Kinney for an activity to quell my nerves. Noting that most people were walking instead of driving, I parked alongside the curb, taking care to triple check the parking rules in this foreign landscape before indulging in a mini-adventure.

The world felt so much more official here.

It wasn't a suburban shopping center animated by stay-at-home moms and businessmen dropping into the neighborhood Starbucks, a sterile merry-go-round of safety within a container of routine.

It was a mosaic sans a single meaning.

I walked south, passing a handful of people more fashionable in their morning coffee garb than I for my interview, calling the visibly stunted pieces of myself into view. Lost in my self-loathing, I all but missed the first signs of congregated life I'd seen.

A clandestine line forming outside an unmarked establishment.

I hopped into the formation propagating down the ramp, debating whether this place was open to the public, wondering if other people could tell how sorely out of place I was. But with the amount of people exiting holding cups labeled *Intelligentsia*, my reservations relaxed.

I passed through the gateway to the atrium of the industrial space with uncharacteristically high ceilings acoustically clashing with the rap music that animated the white walls. Cement rows, replacing tables and chairs, were methodically employed as leveled seating to accommodate the maximum number of people possible within this confined space. The alternative vibe of the baristas (not a transient position but a true Angeleno career) mirrored that of the patrons, all of whom gazed intently into their reflections upon their MacBooks, dusting crumbs from their meticulously maintained lumberjack beards and vintage red lips.

The artistic kaleidoscope of the patronage was earthy but relevant, raw but refined, confident yet hyper-aware.

I removed myself to a distant outlook point from the corner of the highest row, intoxicated by this mysterious slice of life that I had stumbled into all because of an internship I had found on the Internet.

I wanted this.

I wanted to be here, learning from people who clearly knew more than me, graduating to the next level of professionalism.

Doing something as an external manifestation of my inner self.

I left Venice an hour later with an unprecedented certainty. Although my interview was unremarkable, my accidental muffin that morning had changed my life.

LA intrigue was now destiny.

I sat at my desk sweating through my shirt while waiting for the Skype icon to appear on my screen.

This interview was grounds for a panic attack because working for Ranger Productions actually mattered to me.

The iconic ring sounded. Brian was calling.

His face opened onto the screen as he introduced himself. I extended my hand outward, perpendicular to the camera, and moved it up and down.

"Uh, what are you doing?"

"This is a Skype handshake. Nice to meet you."

A smirk made a momentary appearance before quickly proceeding to business.

"Why don't you tell me about yourself?"

He leaned back in his chair, diffusing my anxiety as I continued to speak. He was actually listening.

"So, I don't usually do this, but would you like to be a part of our internship program this summer?"

I restrained the shockwaves of giddiness seeping through my eyes from entering the screen.

"That would be great. Thank you so much."

"I'll email you all the documents."

He returned the Skype handshake before hanging up.

Elated could not describe the insurmountable level of ecstasy shooting out my fingertips. I had to run around the house a few times to dispel the excess exhilaration.

I was going to LA to learn about film.

In order to receive college credit for my internship, I was required to choose a professor as a mentor. I arbitrarily chose a female professor instructing one of my required major courses that quarter.

Denise Lampling.

Until my email requesting her mentorship, she had not known of my existence nor of my attendance in her class. We met in her spacious office skipping prerequisite small talk.

"What is the name of the company? We want to ensure the validity of this internship."

I grinned at her defensive nature.

"Ranger Productions."

She quickly typed it into Google, taking pause to register the amount of popular films they had made.

"Alright. That will work."

She turned to examine me. I smiled and shrugged.

"What do you know about film?"

She rose from her chair without explanation, gliding toward the ceiling-high bookshelves coating the available wall space of her office.

"Well, I took one film class here—"

She placed four large textbooks into my arms.

"Although those aren't exactly what I'm looking for, I'll email you a list of books that I want you to find in the library. You will read those, and I will conduct an oral exam with you on the basis of those books."

I was both flattered and intimidated.

I had never approached a professor before. I had been so preoccupied by my real life outside of school that bonding with professors was playing fourth fiddle, if there ever was such a thing. But, seeing as a mythical sage had yet to bring me the terms of my voyage, I would take any guide I could get.

"Thanks, Professor Lampling."

I stood, cradling the weight of the books in my arms, confused over whether I should leave or stay. She placed her reading glasses on the bridge of her nose and stared into the computer monitor.

"Where are you going to live?"

"Oh, well, I'm from Orange County, so I'll probably just commute."

She chuckled, looking over at me, but my expression did not change.

"Oh. That's not going to work."

"It's not that far."

"Have you ever sat in traffic in Los Angeles?"

"No."

"You need to find a place to live."

"Okay."

"I'll email you the list."

It took me a moment before realizing that *that* was the signal for me to go. I had almost forgotten my manners out of the raw stun of such a brief yet efficient first encounter.

"Thank you again."

Professor Lampling's books welcomed me into the iconic world of film, inhabited by savants and weirdos—the likes of Tarantino and Lynch—whose idiosyncrasies underlined their genius.

There was a hundred-year evolution of cinema that one should be familiar with if they were interested in sounding informed, and luckily I had a few months to gloss over the details.

The universe had launched me back into the galvanic realm of the unknown, but it felt different this time.

The hype was justified.

The First Day of The Rest of My Life

I sat in my car, attempting to control the caffeine shakes before my impending entrance into the shimmering production office situated in the mythical terrain of Santa Monica.

I had arrived at seven a.m. for the nine a.m. Monday morning meeting.

I passed the time arguing with myself over whether I should try to nap or not, an unresolved debate that was eventually broken up by the consistent stream of what looked like other interns—driving similarly shitty cars as mine—pulling into the parking lot. I paused for a few beats so as not to be mistaken for a stalker before following them at a distance along their route to the main building.

The lobby exuded the same cinematic grandeur as a scene in a film. I could feel the audience's voyeuristic gaze of my unreadiness as I tiptoed along the polished granite floor toward the elevator.

I rode up alone, exiting into a darkened lobby, looking left then right at a vacant reception desk. According to the number on the outer window, I was at the correct office.

I slowly crept past the desk, through the abandoned cubicle formation, following the rustling of conversation that led me deeper down a hallway. Framed movie posters of the films they had released adorned the walls. I passed by offices with unrecognizable names accompanied by important titles like *Creative Development* and *Physical Production.*

I consciously reminded myself to stay composed, swallowing my intimidated wonder as I approached the illuminated back half of the office.

Five people were engaged with various tasks on computers within a communal cubicle. Some were reading paper scripts while others were looking online at a website called Deadline.com from their laptops. As I drew closer, what appeared to be a postgraduate-aged gentleman in glasses spotted me from behind a desktop monitor and popped his previously concealed face into view.

"You must be the last of us. I'm Sheldon."

"Nice to meet you. I'm Cee."

"Here, let me show you around."

I apprehensively waved to the others whose attention had been captured by the surprise recruit to the already-formed team, compromising their ability to reciprocate my greeting appropriately.

Sheldon took me by the CEO's office, where his two assistants—both half-awake, using their headsets as counterbalances to their drooping heads—sat. They both politely smiled in my direction, adding another name they needed to memorize to their new-intern list before politely suggesting that Sheldon teach me how to make the CEO's coffee. Sheldon took this direction seriously, stiffening with purpose, as he led me down an indistinct hallway, a clone of all the others.

After my brief tour, I was released back into the pen without further introduction to the other sixteen interns loitering in the intern bay. I straddled the line of observing and staring as the clock struck nine and casual exchange switched to quiet study. A vision of a red carpet unraveling as we all took a knee in preparation for the CEO's grand entrance—cape and crown included—flashed across my mind. But the echo of his steps were disproportionate to the display that emerged. Dressed in jeans and a Lacoste polo, he walked with his gaze intently fixed upon his feet and his iPhone pressed to his ear until he reached his office and closed the door. The tension in the air felt vaguely reminiscent of the hotel. A collective reverence to a figurative god whose power relied upon converting others to believe in said power. The handle latching into place initiated a frenetic outbreak. Some interns hastily grabbed their notebooks and scripts, while others burned the plastic casters of executive chairs against the carpeted hallway into the conference room.

Once within the glass case, stillness assumed control.

Us interns were cast as props, setting the scene for the execs who entered in spurts. They knowingly ignored us, acknowledging one another from their oversized chairs instead. Unlike a traditional performance, a guardedness dictated their subdued interactions until the final exec scurried into the room. The CEO trailed her heels, and a symphonic hush fell.

He assumed command at the head of the desk before addressing his subjects with a smile, an act each face reciprocated his way. His demeanor was light, inquiring what movies we had seen that weekend before moving into business affairs and pitches.

Pitches meant that we would go through a list of scripts that had been submitted to the production company for consideration as a slated project. Both an assistant or executive and an intern would read the same script the week (or days) prior. On the day of the meeting, when the script's name was announced, the assigned intern would summarize the details of the plot, list its genre, compare it to another movie of a similar vein, and describe why the company should or shouldn't consider making it in one to two sentences. Depending on the accuracy of the pitch, the assistant or executive would contribute their insight as well.

But the way I saw it was that each intern had to calmly and concisely make a presentation in front of the whole company, speaking two or three times depending upon how many scripts that intern had read.

I started mentally hyperventilating.

The books I had read in preparation for my internship had not discussed anything about scripts. Plus, almost all sixteen of my

peers were either in film school at various reputable institutions—
USC, Emerson, and LMU—had already graduated, or were
internationally trained—one from Rome, one from Sweden, and
one from England—and were using this internship as a launchpad
for a job.

It was the epitome of life reflecting art.

An off-Broadway show based on a true story of the workplace,
receiving critical acclaim for its stunningly accurate portrayal of
a fish-out-of-water story within the very industry that produces
those stories. It made an unprecedented run, lasting the entirety of
my internship.

That first week, the competition among the team of interns was
palpable.

Whenever an assistant approached the bay, interns transformed
into well-trained dogs: ears perked, salivating for one of the treats
ranging from food runs to script deliveries to research projects. But
even though no one concealed their motivation of recognition, all
sixteen of them were likable. They weren't assholes. They weren't
condescending. They would help each other out based on the
principle of never fucking up because if one of us fucked up, then
we all looked bad. They also knew that it would behoove us to
be nice to one another, laying the groundwork for networking
opportunities in the future.

On my second day, the second assistant asked another intern,
Joan, to accompany me on my first lunch run.

We had forty-five minutes to get across town to Century City to
pick up the phone order before the lunch meeting at one p.m. We
were also given specific instructions to ensure that one of the salads
was dry with an extra order of chicken and a side of balsamic
vinegar and olive oil.

Joan drove while I read her directions from the Google Maps
printout.

"So, how'd you get the internship?"

It was the first real interaction I was having with one of the other interns. I had been keeping to myself as best I could to avoid blowing my cover.

"I applied through a website called Entertainmentcareers.com. You?"

"Cool. You know Remy? Yeah, she and I have known each other forever. And she knows Ray Romano's niece, who had an internship here, so she helped us get in."

"Cool."

I had just assumed that other people had gotten in on merit alone, but nothing in the industry is ever as it seems. Nor is there any justice system. Either you get lucky, know someone, or prepare to work long and hard in order to accomplish the two aforementioned criteria.

We pulled up to the trendy café that was fashionably inaccessible. It was the only storefront embedded within a residential area on the edge of an eight-lane street. Steel-poled gargoyles labeled *30 minute parking* protected suburban families from hungry souls lingering too long.

Joan had no choice but to drop me off and drive in circles around the block until we synced up again. I checked my phone. We had fifteen minutes to get back, and it had taken us thirty to get there. I ran in, pushing my way through the augmented, self-important faces squeezed into the uncomfortable foyer to approach the counter. Upon hearing the name, the disgruntled employee pivoted to grab the gleaming brown paper bag. I glanced inside, confirming that the dressing was on the side, paid, and ran toward Joan's car as she turned the corner when the assistant called me.

"Where are you guys? You need to be here, *now!*"

"I know. I'm sorry. We're on our way."

She let out a frustrated groan before hanging up.

"Don't worry," Joan said, "She didn't give us enough time. It's not our fault."

Joan dropped me off in front of the building, arriving ten minutes after one. I ran through the lobby, pausing for the elevator, and burst through the doors toward the conference room.

But no one was there.

I was looking around all the while trying to steady my breath as the second assistant bumped into me from behind.

"Finally!"

She snatched the plastic carrier bags out of my hands, throwing them onto the distinguished conference table to examine each order.

"Why is there bread in here?"

"What do you mean?"

"He can't have bread. Get rid of this."

She threw me the bread.

There was not a trash receptacle within sight, yet I hesitated walking out, confused whether I was supposed to stay until she released me or not. She finally noticed my stiffened state, a misplaced Royal British Guard.

"You're good to go."

She was still wearing her headset, the terms of her employment reflected back at me.

We were all easily replaceable.

L ike a shadow, silent and empty from the overpowering of my gears to be prepared at any moment to be the best I could be, I would return to my dark and barren quarters on the bottom floor of the USC house I was subletting.

Since I didn't know anyone or any groovy place to go, I dedicated this time in LA to absorbing a variety of TV and film on Netflix and reading any scripts that were available, whether they were films we were currently producing or ones that were seeking a home.

I would have lots to debrief my professor on at our first appointment since starting my internship, which happened to land on the same day as my first pitch.

The meeting progressed in the same fashion as the last, upbeat and rudimentary, except that I was the only one in the room visibly experiencing hypertension, obsessing over the details of my presentation, mentally comparing the exemplary pitches that some interns gave to the ones that made everyone in the room cringe.

Would the CEO ask me a question?

Would we joke?

Would he expect me to provide a secondary comparison to another film on the spot?

The CEO announced the name of the script.

I nervously cleared my throat, smiling and nodding in his direction, keenly aware that mine was the freshest face in the group, as if he had noticed or even cared.

"*Cirque de Littles*," I began, "is an interpretation of what would have happened to the famous midget family from *Wizard of Oz* if they had never left the circus."

I could feel the energy in the room shift, but I proceeded anyway. I wanted to get my initiation over with as quickly as possible.

"It focuses on the midgets' ignorance of the politically incorrect treatment they endured during that time period."

The CEO chimed in, "You mean *little person*," guiding me in the right direction.

But I took it as a setup.

"Exactly!" I said, employing the use of air quotes to emphasize what I had assumed was a joke, "'*Little person*.'"

I continued to use the word *midget* for about thirty more seconds before he waved me off.

"Doesn't sound like a film we would ever make. Let's move on."

During lunch with my professor later that day, I recounted my pitch, emphasizing how the CEO had cut me off.

"You used the word," she peered around before dropping to a

whisper, "*midget* in front of the entire company?!"
"Yeaaahhh..."
"Cee! That's like using the 'n' word!"

Ohhhh.

That's why he had interrupted me.

"The Earles family are well-known figures. I discussed the film Freaks in the class I taught about disability in film at NYU."

I was still wearing yoga pants at this toga party.

She moved on.
"Have you found a place to live yet?"
"I'm subletting a place at USC until July."
"Okay. I spoke with my husband, and it's okay if you stay in our back house for the summer. All we ask is that you catsit for us when we go on vacation."
"Wait. What? You live in LA?"
"My husband, Jim, is a professor at UCLA. We also have a house in Venice with a guest house in the back. You can stay there."
I was trying to make sense of this unwarranted gesture of generosity.
"But I can pay you."
"No. Don't pay us. Just take care of the cat."
Lunch was over.
She got up, and we parted ways into our separate vehicles. She always had this authoritatively abrupt yet gentle way of moving on to the next thing.
I followed her car through the Venice Canals as she guided me down Washington Boulevard so I could find the 405 on-ramp. Driving through the rare occurrence of no traffic permitted a spontaneous shower of tears that fogged the windows of my eyes.

The pendulum of favor and reward had finally swung back in my direction.

71

Without the financial commitment of rent, I could live off my savings for the summer.

I would also be closer to Santa Monica so I could spend less time sitting in traffic and more time exploring Los Angeles, reading scripts, and close-watching films.

But, most of all, she said **I would be living in Venice.**

Excuse me?

Venice?

The place I fell in love with.

The place I promised myself I would return to one day.

The gods were shining down their light and it was my duty to compensate for my pitiful first impression by working to deliver a more coherent front. But since each facet of my current situation was new, it was impossible to process and integrate every component all at once.

Flashes of concern for how others perceived me would momentarily knock me out.

I wanted to be the assistants' preferred intern. I wanted the execs to know my name because they saw my potential all the while converting my fellow interns' indifference into support.

I trod cautiously through the rest of my first month, focusing my attention on every available interaction that crossed my path, whether it was between two execs or an assistant and an intern. I developed my own way of determining which qualities, actions, and information to take away from each individual in the office by who and how they received it.

For instance, the notably reliable interns were easy to distinguish because the assistants would look lost if they had an assignment and none of them were there. These interns were not annoying or entitled, condescending or adulating. They did things without asking questions and accomplished them efficiently.

Although I knew it would take a balanced mixture of patience and practice to arrive at my desired destination, I did not know how to embrace that journey. I had a tendency to rankle the process with my mind. Every time I felt less than worthy—irrespective of whether I had made a mistake or not—I admonished myself for any shortcoming I could easily latch onto. This rendition of anxiety was different from what I had derived from the hotel though. Instead of debilitating, it was inspiring.

LA Magic

One evening after work had finished, the company held a panel for the interns in one of the conference rooms.

The CEO and his assistants, a producer and her assistant, and, of course, Brian, all graced us with their distinct paths that had led them to the present at Ranger.

While listening to the condensed versions of their life stories, the inner workings of the industry began to concretize. Apart from two, they had all worked at a talent agency before branching into more niche specific positions. Meaning no one could expect to have a job handed to them by virtue of being an intern at Ranger. We were expected to get more extensive training within an agency, where we would start in the mailroom, familiarizing ourselves with the names of the multiple hands that belonged to the array of divisions within each studio that worked with whichever agency that had chosen us, the exclusive recipients of glorified indentured servitude.

The CEO was the odd-man out, having stumbled upon the Academy Award–winning script that put him on the map in the same way Aladdin had stumbled upon the lamp.

The script was his pillar of excellence, continually referenced, revealing facts previously unknown.

Not only had it been the screenwriter's first script, but he had been living in Ohio while working a nine-to-five he hated prior to its submission to a screenplay competition.

It all felt connected.

My position at my internship existed because of the amount of scripts submitted. Production companies were always looking for material, but employees didn't have the time necessary to sift through all the shit. The majority of scripts I was reading— scripts represented by agents—were stories about contrived characters, formulaic character arcs, and empty dialogue. It was incomprehensible how the amount of good material being produced was direly disproportionate to the amount of available material. And the more I read, the more I thought to myself that I too could write something that could win an award someday.

O ver the Fourth of July, my parents invited me to spend the weekend with them, but, still craving healthy separation, I had made other plans.

In my strategic absence, my family decided to stop at a local beach spot they had never been to where my mother recognized an old boyfriend whom she hadn't seen since middle school.

Story goes that they were catching up when my mother mentioned that her eldest child was living in LA as a film intern. Rather than reverence at such dazzling information, he raised my mom's revelation with one of his own. His brother-in-law was also in film, working as an agent at one of the top five agencies (a string of letters that did not elevate nor diminish the previously noted information). My mom, expressing the appropriate response of astonishment, was then prompted for her email address so he could introduce me to his brother-in-law, which is how I spent an hour inside one of the most premiere offices in the industry.

Once I received the email, I researched said brother-in-law to discover that he casually represented both actors and writers such as Tobey Maguire, Joseph Gordon-Levitt, and Diablo Cody.

Yet another bizarre stroke of synchronicity.

I had been researching this La Femme group of female screenwriters that included Dana Fox, Lorene Scafaria, Elizabeth

Meriwether, and Diablo Cody because Professor Lampling had
mentioned that she was old friends with Lorene Scafaria's mom.

The fact that this established agent would take a meeting with an
unremarkable intern, whose etiquette on political correctness was
questionable and level of savvy nonexistent, boggled my mind. I
kept news of the event to myself and went into the meeting without
anything substantial prepared beyond my eager smile and profuse
perspiration.

The polished cold marble of the lobby where visitors were
directed to sit and wait at the other end of the room from
reception accomplished its intent.

The only other person waiting fidgeted, pacing around, before
anxiously turning around to plop down next to me, attempting to
distract himself with his cell phone. He was dressed in street clothes,
holding a skinny leather portfolio under his other arm. I could only
imagine how much more nervous a person could be than me, and
I wasn't even expected to present my life's work to the prestigious
magistrates of talent.

After twenty minutes—my pits having reached a visible degree
of wetness—I was finally met by the brother-in-law's assistant. She
led me down the hallway, engaging me in rudimentary pleasantries,
before pausing in front of the doors that separated the extremities
from the heart. Using the retractable cord, she scanned her badge
against the wall. The formerly bland doors uncharacteristically
sparkled, ceremoniously widening, a blinding light infusing the
doorway. I followed her through the portal, sucking me into a
world I could not separate from the way I regarded it in my head.

Lifeless rows of cubicles were occupied by tired faces strapped
into headsets robotically multi-tasking. Their desktops served as
both the means and diversion away from the invisible shackles that
bound them to an incessant flow of work.

As I walked by, these former interns must have known exactly
who I was by my poor fashion sense and permanent gawk face. A
few of them caught my eye, not to judge me but to telepathically

message me.

Save yourself. It isn't what you think it is.

But I could not objectively perceive their unideal circumstances because I was too blinded by where their paths had already led them.

Validation.

The brother-in-law was finishing up a call and motioned for me to take a seat when we arrived. He was throwing around a few big names and why they wouldn't be right for the part into his Bluetooth earbud, swiveling the chair to face out his Century City window.

Distantly placed on the opposite side of the room on the guest sofa, I was figuratively pinching myself to never forget these moments. Moments where I had nothing to lose but felt so unequipped to be where I was.

He hung up soon thereafter, easily segueing out of a business call into a comforting handshake. He got on my level, taking a seat in the strategically posited chair across from me, inviting me to tell him a little more about myself.

The moment I had been waiting for. The unequivocal opportunity to divulge my fluency in strife with someone powerful enough to hire me.

I briefly prefaced where I went to school and how I had worked full-time to help support my family these past couple years, but he didn't flinch. No sympathy. No greater interest. He was simply waiting for what came next.

"So finding film has been a godsend. It's the first time that the world makes sense to me."

And then it came.

The knowing smile.

The youthful reflection of one's past self seated before them confirming that they had fully transitioned into the expert.

"I'm immersing myself as much as possible with the aspirations of writing for Hollywood someday."

Where did that come from?

How was he the first person I would ever voice that to?

He encouraged me to hold to the path, read and write and read and write (that's what they all say), before offering me one piece of advice that stuck.

"Never let anybody forget you. Now, don't be annoying, because I'm very busy, but don't be afraid to remind me that you're still around. We like helping others, but you have to be willing to hold up your end, too."

He briefly shared his origin story of having graduated from the mailroom, which has since been renamed *The Training Program*, earlier than all his counterparts.

"The president handpicked me without considering other assistants first. I still, to this day, can't figure out why. I was learning on the go, making as few mistakes as humanly possible—"

Dedication laced every word.

He was not in it for the celebrity, the glamour, or the fame. He was a product of the race, enlivened by the challenge to turn contracts with countless moving parts into a reality.

My gratitude was ineffable.

He had graciously offered me the coveted gift that most industry players would unapologetically disregard lending.

Time.

A s I walked back into my internship that afternoon, I happened to pass by the CEO in the hall when he stopped me.

"Hey. Why didn't you tell me you had a meeting with Gene today?"

"Uh…"

"It's good to tell me those things. Gene and I go way back."

He put his hand on my shoulder, smiling reassuringly.

"I will next time."

He walked off, resuming his life, unaware of how affected I had been by the last two hours of mine.

I had only started a month ago, and, all of a sudden, an executive and an agent were discussing the likes of me.

A plan for the future was being aroused from its slumber.

If I saw myself as a screenwriter, as a creative player in this industry, how did I get there?

I spent the next two months reading, refining, and making friends with as many of my peers and assistants that I could.

By the time summer came to a close, I was the last intern standing, and the duty of transitioning the incoming fall tadpoles—grooming them to express dominant traits during their internships—fell to me. I turned the morsels of advice I had learned along the way into an informational packet, hoping to save them the time and self-doubt it had taken me three months to shed.

21

A week before my internship ended, it was my twenty-first birthday. The thirtieth of August two-thousand and eleven.

I woke up early on the morning of the thirty-first in a hospital bed to the unmistakable sensation of my foot being tickled with a pencil and a subtle voice singing, "*Minnamow, Minnamow.*"

I blinked heavily, my vision assessing what lay before me.

The bald man in a nurse's uniform at the foot of the bed came into view first. It was a bed with poles for arms that had tubes wrapping around it. Tubes that flowed into my veins.

I felt myself look to the left where I saw my mother. I blinked to zoom in on her bloodshot eyes, still tearing, as she squeezed my hand. I am sure she was gasping and repeating *thank you,* but I couldn't help but turn back toward the nurse.

"Huh?"

"Minnamow is the name of my dog."

How was that relevant?

All of a sudden, he accelerated into full-throttle mode, an aggressive shift from the gentle voice I had awoken to.

"You're never gonna do that again, are you? **Are you?** Gonna hurt yourself like that. That's not fair to anyone, most especially your loving mother."

I had no idea what he meant.

I felt like I had been pressed between two cement walls that had been moving closer and closer together, from which I clearly had not escaped, and passed out from shock. I was beyond disoriented. I could not recall much of my birthday. The last thing I remember was a blow job shot at Mammalia with a few friends from college.

My mom explained the rest to me, as best she could, without crying or swallowing her words.

"Dad came to pick Melissa and you up from the bar. When you got in the car, you fell asleep, and by the time you got home, you wouldn't wake up. We dropped Melissa off, and your dad and I took you to the ER. You were unconscious and unresponsive, for about five hours. Then, finally, you threw up."

Without directly saying it, my mom was telling me that I had put myself into a self-induced coma.

"Cee, how much did you have to drink?"

I had enough default sense to know not to relay that once, in college, I had taken fifteen shots. I only know the quantity because the next morning I woke up with hash marks written along the inside of my arm.

No, I could not admit that.

I could not admit that I had drunk way past my limit countless times before, arousing from drunken stupors on people's lawns, yet without alcohol poisoning. I was not boasting. Based on my history of consumption, I had deduced that I possessed a tolerance that lasted up to a certain point, at which I would fall asleep.

"I had some wine with you guys. Then I had a shot of 151 and a blow job shot. That's all I can remember."

"Your BAC was two-point-oh. You had poisoning and were almost at the lethal level."

My mind was racking for an answer.

"Mom, it couldn't have been."

"How could a hospital test result be incorrect?"

Now was not the time to argue. I wasn't in any state to negotiate the gravity of the situation. I just wanted to sleep.

When we got home, I crawled into my bed beside Melissa. "Hey. You're okay!" she gleefully exclaimed.

"Dude, what happened?"

"I don't know. You seemed fine to me. You made out with Joe."

"What?!?!"

"Yeah. You don't remember that? That was pretty early on."

"Mel. No. I should not have done that. I would have never done that even if I was drunk."

"I don't know. But I'm so glad you're okay!"

Melissa left an hour later, leaving me to my own faulty devices to crack the case that no one was going to solve on my behalf.

I texted another friend who had been there for a few hours.

"Dude, you probably got roofied. Mammalia is known for doing that."

I looked up how Rophynol is processed in your body and how it is tested.

> **The toxic effects of Rophynol are aggravated by concurrent use of alcohol.**

That applied to me.

> **A urine test can detect the presence of Rohypnol up to sixty hours after ingestion. Rohypnol can be more difficult to detect than similar drugs because it is in low concentrations and is cleared quickly by the body.**

That is why they did not find it on my tests.

I sauntered out of my room, having felt no better by discovering the reason behind my admittance into the ER on the night of what is supposed to be a memorable celebration of joviality.

My parents were watching TV when I stepped in front of it and broke down into tears.

"I am so sorry. I didn't mean to..."

My mom took me into her arms.

"We know, sweetie. We know. We're just glad you are okay."
Yet again, no one had texted me.

No one had been there for me besides Melissa—who hadn't
noticed anything strange—and my parents—who had luckily
intervened to ensure the safety of my life.

I explained to them that I hadn't known that Mammalia had
a reputation for bartenders that spiked drinks, and I guess I had
gotten unlucky last night.

My mom didn't believe me.

"But mom, there is no way my BAC would be that high with what I
drank. It doesn't make sense."

"Honey, you drank 151."

I could not tell her it had been my second time being roofied in
two years. That was something I kept to myself, something I had
survived yet would never have predicted as a potential reoccurrence.

Senior Year

Even though it was my last year of school, I made the calculated decision to go back to living with my parents.

For as much as managing their toxic energy was still a mystery to me, I needed any financial break I could get while looking into working for the hotel again to replenish my savings.

Despite my lack of experience, I applied for a cocktail server position and, somehow, the timing of their desperate need for employees continued to align with someone's memory of my competence.

I got the job and was back in the two places where it had all began.

It was only October when the second assistant to the CEO from Ranger reached out.

> *Hey! How have you been? I just wanted to be the first to let you know that Natalia's leaving because I would love for you to interview for my position after I take hers!*

Yes, this really happened.

I had finally received the invitation that would vindicate my past and validate me all at the same time.

Yet some internal force was preventing me from pursuing it.
I shared the news with Professor Lampling.

"You have to take this job. Don't worry about your classes. I'll email all of your professors. Just take it."

Logically speaking, she was right. An opportunity that was too good to be true had presented itself. But, deep inside of me, I knew that a job would be there when I was ready for it despite the social discourse otherwise.

Both my parents and the assistant understood my decision to finish my degree before pursuing a professional venture, but my professor was not as quick to relinquish her stance.

"You can finish your degree on the side."

True, I *could* do that, but after having observed the CEO's assistants for three months—the first people in the office and the last to leave—I could not justify sacrificing my welfare for my professional advancement any longer. For as much as I held hope for my future in film, I longed for a reprieve. This professional archetype of pounding the pavement to get where you wanted to be as fast as your feet could take you had already begun to take its toll.

The prospect of a career rattled my psyche, causing unfulfilled wishes to fall from the highest shelves.

Going abroad hit me on the head, a timely rustle that allowed me to work through the residual doubt from rejecting a secure job by researching opportunities studying abroad instead. But, of course, none of the programs offered Argentina (my country of choice) during winter quarter or were funded through the university. After scraping through every possible configuration, I applied for the single program that was compatible with my situation, assuming that I would be able to afford the eleven-thousand-dollar program fee with my financial aid package.

Confirmation of whether or not this course would become my path would not arrive until January, ensuing a period of life when the fluid stream of work, school, and home provoked my relationship with existentialism.

I was not suffering from overwhelm like my first time moving home as much as I was grappling with the confusion over how life worked.

My summer hiatus from painful memories had given me enough perspective to realize that it was not my heart that was generating my anxiety as much as it was my environment. Returning to the tangible manifestation of what can happen if one does not realize monetary success highlighted this newfound connection.

I inherently disagreed with the steep paradigm that money dictated happiness.

If I could have the most validating summer of my life exhausting my savings, then what people were doing for a living had to be the true culprit of discontent, not a lack of money.

But since my parents were in the same place of aching for a financial windfall as when I had left, I had returned to the same place of depending on high-rollers to rack up expensive tabs and tip 25 percent. At the end of the night, we servers would share the sum of our individual earnings, the lowly lot deliberately coveting the lives of ease those we served must have, narrowing the wage gap by comparing our arbitrary income among ourselves.

Living in this tainted reality crystallized summer's overwhelming brilliance into a dream.

Three months away was not long enough to knock my worldview up into the next level of understanding. It had simply been a glimpse into the way life *could* be. The way money, hearts, fate, and willpower wove together after a period of feeling like the loom of life was permanently broken. Life in LA had been the beacon of truth. The light I was chasing to become my norm even though it felt distant and hallucinatory because nothing else in my life had changed. The collective strength of my corruptive surroundings was pulling me back into the invisible pressures of work and home.

To be enough and have enough increased my density, frustration congested my chest, which is how I began smoking to take off the edge.

I would sneak into the garage to take a hit in peaceful secrecy while everyone was in bed, so by the time I returned to my room, the effects had already taken place. It was the only sliver of my day when a smile would effortlessly emerge, and my inner being would bounce with the buoyancy of a child, without regard for anything "real."

Since I often smoked alone, the mental liberation of pot didn't catch up to me until my consciousness anchored, encouraging me to recount my day back to myself. The fog of loneliness would roll in as I came down, mourning my temporary comfort with being alone. I could not transcend my sober limitations with my high sense of allowing, but writing slowly unraveled both the diagnosis and the cure.

I began journaling, transcribing previously unspoken thoughts and emotions, materializing my inner world. Although I could taste the metallic warmth in my mouth, the benefits of the clarity generated on the page starkly outweighed the pain.

The overall discovery was **I was as content as I could be**.

How underwhelming is that?

I was twenty-one, rating my life on the notch above apathy.

For as much as I could see things differently, more than that had yet to change.

T he only person I saw regularly was Scout, a friend from freshman year with whom I had reconnected.

On my days off, I would drive to San Diego for class, ceremoniously ending the night at his bro-pad with Whole Foods sandwiches and homegrown herb.

Over the following two hours, the rare thought regions of our minds spontaneously ejaculated alter egos, synchronicities, and spiritual connections. Whether we were on the roof, transfixed by the stars, or acting out a scene as a couple who erupts into an argument while making dinner, life felt surreally authentic.

He was the only outlet that did not challenge who I was or what I thought, giving me enough confidence to explore my self-expression.

The way men were salaciously ogling me—at work or otherwise—spawned a visceral reaction, and I didn't know how to take a stand.

At what point did I cross the line from being polite to defending myself?

My breaking point came when I went to Scout's house to hang out after one of his midterms. He was discussing the exam with another student from his class, who paid no notice to me until Scout introduced us. He scanned me up and down, taking in the fact that I had my Greek letters on.

"So you're a transfer student?"

"No. I got in the same as you."

"Oh."

According to this friend, I did not look smart enough to get into school the same way he had.

There had to be some way for me to dictate how other people interpreted my existence.

So, I did something drastic.

I cut off my hair.

My luscious brunette armor that had protected me since age fifteen.

It was impulsive and covert. I went to my hair stylist one evening when I was supposed to be locked away in my room, studying for finals. Shortly after I returned, I was sitting in my room when my dad knocked to come in. He opened the door and did a double take before laughing from shock at the pixie cut that remained.

"Oh my god. Does your mom know?"

I smiled and shook my head. He shook his head back in disbelief, laughing, as he closed the door.

I took his subliminal invitation literally and decided to go show my mom.

I walked up the stairs as she was walking across the second-floor hall to her room. She caught sight of my haircut from the banister, slowly shook her head, and continued along her trajectory with a single forced breath of exasperation.

It felt right.

I was getting reactions from people in spite of my appearance rather than in regard to it. I had made a gesture that held purpose and meant something to me, something continually shown to me by life that I wanted to embody.

Nothing is what it seems to be.

The week after finals, I received the email regarding the one scholarship I qualified for to study abroad.

I had been granted twenty-five hundred dollars.

I had never been awarded money like that before, especially money based on an essay highlighting my experiences at home despite my domestic aching to go abroad.

However, the excitement lasted but a moment.

Financial aid would not cover the extra nine thousand dollars for the program fee nor could my parents supplement the funding. So as quickly as that cloud of a dream entered into my life, it blew away to help someone else along their journey.

I returned to the drawing board, waving goodbye to life abroad, pondering what my next step after graduation should be.

What Is Love?

I entered 2012 practicing conscious breathing into the nuances of my psyche, fueling the rebellious fire in my belly when an unforeseen opportunity to act on who I was becoming presented itself.

My best friends from childhood invited me to an M83 Concert in LA. But, more importantly, they were wondering whether or not I was going to join in the contraband culture of the night.

I teetered, wary of experiencing this unknown sensation I had heard stories of countless times. But, seeing as my route to escapism upon a jet plane had yet to present itself, this alternate route via my two best friends and Scout—who I asked to be the designated driver on my first transport into the (sometimes) wonderland of drugs—appeared to be where I was supposed to be instead.

We were among the first in the venue, entering an hour early. With the lights at full temperature, the twelve of us weren't the most discreet, loitering by the bathrooms, rumbling over when we were going to take **it**.

A few of the more seasoned players looked at their cell phones, calculating how long it would take for the capsule to release, as I stood by with a dearth of illegal substance prowess and zoned out. I had lost track of the conversation when Jen pulled me back into my body, grabbing my hand, following Lucy into the bathroom without saying a word. They filed into separate stalls, so I did the same.

Lucy whispered to me through the crack of the barrier.

"Make sure to gently bite into them before you swallow."

I had two capsules of molly tucked safely in my jean pocket.

Thrill surged through my veins, making the most minute task of taking the pills out of my pocket difficult. I unearthed them, employing as much force as I could so as not to keep Lucy and Jen waiting. I balanced the remaining capsule in my sweaty palm, placing the first subject between the back of my teeth, slightly squeezing it, before dry swallowing. I repeated the same with the second pill before flushing the toilet to finish the charade.

The girls weren't speaking, teasing their hair at the roots with their fingernails when I opened the stall door. I started to wash my hands when Jen yanked me again, thrusting me back into the formless night.

The rest of the group incrementally trickled in, mostly in pairs, until we had reassembled our original formation. We were standing in a makeshift circle, distracting ourselves with surface chatter amidst compulsive sips of beer, anticipating more than just the band to take the stage.

During the opening act, I had unconsciously stopped willing myself to feel something when it happened.

The lights jumped from side to side, arousing nerve endings I had never before felt engage. The sound I had once called music had been reformatted into a tangible sensation of love; a language I inherently understood but had never before tapped into.

The music stopped as the lights rose. I thought I was going to cry. I pivoted around to look at Jen and Lucy, shell-shocked.

"Wait! It's over?"

They both chuckled and shared a knowing glance.

"You're totally there, huh?"

I realized what they meant.

"Don't worry," Jen reassured me, "It was just the opener."

She handed me a piece of gum.

"You don't want to grind your teeth."

The novelty of this drug—a drug that can make you feel so certain of something beyond the banality of routine—had not done any of my friends' descriptions justice.

I was lightly gliding through a realm beyond normalcy with the inarguable sense that I belonged. Whole and connected, dropping into a meaningful level of depth with those around me was not only commonplace, it was reciprocated.

At any chance between songs, one of my friends and I would make eye contact and hold it, knowing what the other was thinking and feeling, ending this silent transaction with the safety of a hug, solidifying the embrace with an *I love you*.

Scout and I didn't drive back until two a.m. that night, soaring down the seldom-vacant I-5 freeway. *Levels* by Avicii amplified the coursing drug through the speakers. The wind danced through the windows, tickling our skin. Neither worry nor fear, responsibility nor obligation could touch us. We had reached the pinnacle of the word *alive*.

A fter struggling to sleep, I awoke slightly more sober but with greater insight into my being.

I had been so wound up that I could feel the figurative twine I had bound myself within loosen. Hope was no longer a mirage of the distant future. It was the formerly invisible tether pulling me forward through time.

Zeitgeist resounded through my head.

I felt like a representative of life, an observer of the times. Once having been a skeptic of drugs and, now, participating in the ever-growing mainstream practice of the youth.

I had considered drugs to be evil and synthetic because of the way they could alter one's state of mind so drastically. Nothing that did that could be considered a healthy way to experience reality. Yet both marijuana and ecstasy had enhanced my way of seeing the world, both during and after the fact. It had confirmed my connection to a force unseen. Call it *intuition* or *consciousness*, but I was able to hover outside myself and see the pieces of my life as a play and I as the playwright.

I could decide how I wanted things to be—manifest them—all the while striving for presence in the moment, addressing other stunted facets of my being as they arose, until the way I envisioned my life happening physically manifested into my visual reality at the proper intersection of space and time.

E arlier that week, my last quarter of college had begun. Since I had already met all the requirements for my degree, I just needed to satisfy the unit count to graduate. Which is how my final quarter of college consisted of two dance classes, a gospel choir class, a class on the works of Tolkien, and an acting class.

N ot having considered proximity when arranging my schedule, I broke out into a run across campus once I realized I was late.

I rushed into the theatre building, actively scanning the doorways, searching for the room number, before hastily throwing open the door. Fifteen students silently seated on the floor filling out a paper appeared in front of me. Every pair of eyes darted over their shoulders to gaze upon the delinquent disrupting their concentration.

"You must be Cee."

I focused in on the voice that sung my name.

It had come from a boy. A boy that did not belong at UCSD. An all-American boy with sandy blonde hair, a crystal smile, and steady blue eyes. I was blushing, caught off guard to find someone so attractive in my class.

"Uh, yeah."

"Here. We're filling this out right now."

He was my teacher?
But that couldn't be.
He was so young.

I filled out the form, half-distracted by the striking elephant in the room, rushing to complete it before we went around the circle and shared our answers.

Every other student was majoring in some technical pursuit and had chosen this class to fulfill their art credit. Everyone except me.

"I want to be a screenwriter in LA after I graduate, so I'm in this class to experience the other side of it."

"Nice!" exclaimed the teaching assistant.

Trevor was his name.

Supposedly, TA's taught the entry-level undergraduate acting courses, which made sense. This ragtag bunch didn't need much more than that. And neither did I.

His enthusiastic approval of my dreams was magnetizing.

It was as if I had found that AA battery for the remote when randomly opening a kitchen drawer. It's a long shot to think that I'd actually find one that was unused. But here it was, and I was confident that my heart would not spoil an encounter as unexpected as this.

In terms of my impending graduation, I was not ready for the real world yet.

Although studying abroad was no longer an option, I could not suppress my craving to experience what lies beyond these American borders. My grand-big was working as an au pair overseas while my big sis had earned an international sales position with an oil company. The envy over the presumable ease of their roads, sending them to foreign lands, simmered within.

How could I create a similar version of reality?

Regina and I patched things up soon after my dramatic rejection of our friendship the year prior.

Although we weren't as close as we once were, we still got

together on campus for coffee or lunch occasionally.

I was voicing my inner conflict over the future to her during one of our meet-ups when she randomly suggested that I teach English abroad.

"What? Like in Asia? No. I don't want to do that."

"My TA did it. He said you make really good money and have lots of free time to explore."

"It seems stupid. Teaching my own language?"

She shrugged, and we moved on to another matter. But, little did either of us know, Regina had planted a seed.

Later that day, without much thought, I typed *teach english spanish speaking country* into Google.

The top result was for the program *TEACH*.

It looked reputable: classy font, high resolution images, not too busy with ads and/or archaic icons of a Clip Art professor with wacky hair and glasses, dancing from side to side.

I browsed through their locations.

They operated throughout Spain in a variety of capacities. But the only thing I knew about Spain could be construed from Facebook.

> *Photos of drunken high school friends stumbling around discotecas propped up by other Americans while studying abroad.*

I had no idea what the culture was like, the food, the people, or the historical sites. I was resistant to the idea of copying other people who had gone to Spain to party because that was not why I wanted to go abroad. My goal was to have as few American friends as possible, learn how to speak Spanish fluently, and have adventures.

I reluctantly saved it as a bookmark—a backup—in case I couldn't find a program in Argentina. But the Argentinian programs were not accepting submissions for teachers at that time, and TEACH was.

So I applied to TEACH in Spain, using the two months before their decision would be disclosed to lure in Trevor.

A couple weeks into the quarter, I reached out to him via email about discussing an assignment during office hours.

He responded within the day, suggesting we meet on campus later that week, indirectly releasing a flood of butterflies into my stomach, cleansing my gut of the years of anxious tension laced with depression.

We met at a café on campus with a sparse patronage, taking a seat outside on the cold metal patio chairs, talking square until I asked him to tell me about himself. He started on the surface, rambling about his deep-rooted passion for the Bruins but his indifference toward LA as a city when we finally dug deep enough for him to accidentally reveal something to me.

"My parents don't really get what I'm doing though. I don't think they've ever had dreams like me."

"Well, have you ever asked them?"

He considered this.

"No. I actually haven't."

He did not ask me too many questions, but I did not invite him to either. I never let the dust of our words settle and sink in because I was eager to know everything about him and for him to see, by nature of my attention to him, how great I was as well. The meeting ended, and we had not discussed anything about class but had agreed to exchange one of my favorite indie movies for one of his favorite plays, taking the first step in our relationship.

I was feeling better than I had in a long time.

I had social contact with Regina and Scout outside of class.

I had a love interest.

My job was not as destructive as it had been in the past.

And I was finally going abroad.

Scout and I had planned a spring break trip to Mexico—my graduation present to myself—that ended on the same day that I would receive word from TEACH regarding my acceptance or not.

Trevor emailed the class, reminding us to return any plays that he had loaned out during the quarter at the final the next day.

I still had his play from our coffee date a few weeks back and decided that this was my opportunity to formalize my attraction to him. I wrote him a note and slipped it inside the cover of the play.

> *Hey! It was nice getting to know you. Now that I have graduated, it would be a shame if we didn't stay in touch. Text me (555) 555-5555.*

> *-Cee*

He had broken us up into pairs about two months prior, so we could use the majority of the quarter to prepare the scenes we would be giving as our final. My scene was an open interpretation from *Waiting for Godot*. The setting of a park bench where two homeless men philosophized life had been reappropriated to a college dorm room with a stoner and neurotic roommate as Vladimir and Estragon, respectively.

I excused myself to the bathroom after my performance, the physical stall transforming into a container for my obsessive thoughts as I latched the door.

> *I don't even know what just happened.*

> *I'm so glad I never have to do that in front of him again.*

> *Oh my god! I still have to give him his play back.*

By the time I was washing my hands, the sound of a toilet flushing revealed that I wasn't alone. One of my classmates—whom I had not socialized with at all during class—approached the basin beside me.

"My scene was terrible!"

"No it wasn't. You did great!"

There was an awkward pause, as if she knew that I was just saying that because it was what I was supposed to say.

"Pssh. Trevor doesn't like me." Her gaze met my reflection in the mirror. "But, he sure likes you."

Other people think that he likes me?

"Uh. I don't know."

"Oh, yes he does. Everyone knows it."

I smiled politely, opening the door, so we could leave the awkwardness of this accidental revelation behind closed doors.

After the scenes had ended, we had a class party consisting of obligatory store-bought sugar cookies and forced interaction. We localized in the center of the room, where the same annoyingly happy girl who organized the party was reminiscing about the quarter.

"Trevor, why didn't you ever do one of the exercises with us?"

Trevor just shrugged, employing the cookie as a blockade for a better response.

But the girl kept going.

"Treevoorr!" She let out a playful squeal that allowed her to think. "You should do a kissing scene!"

The energy immediately shifted, spines sat more erect, as she vigorously scanned the room eventually catching my eye.

"With Cee!"

Trevor and I snapped our heads toward one another and immediately looked away upon eye contact.

What the fuck?

People finally began packing up, bidding their adieus while I dawdled as best I could without being obvious. Slowly looking through different pockets of my backpack as if I still hadn't found what I was looking for.

Once the room was empty, I self-consciously shuffled over to the door, acting as nonchalant as possible, passing by the place he had occupied for the last three minutes.

"Thanks for everything," I said.

"Yep! It was a great class."

I quickly snapped the play from behind my back. I had strategically placed the note so it was slightly sticking out from the inside cover. He looked down, catching a peek, and I shoved it into his outreached hand, fleeing from the room before anything else could happen.

On the day before I left, a new text message from an unknown number was waiting in my inbox.

> **Unknown Number:** *Hey! It's Trevor! Sorry, I've been busy with finals. How did they go for you?*

Oh. My. God.

He texted me.

I wanted to jump out of my clothes and run through the halls rejoicing at my belief having been validated.

I told him we should get together after I got back from Mexico, and we set a date. A prospect I was almost more excited for than my first trip ever outside the country.

My dad picked me up from the airport in San Diego upon my return.

I had been without internet for five days, so when we got home, I surged into my room to check my computer for an email from TEACH.

I logged into my email as quickly as I could.

Congratulations—

That was all I needed to see.

My life was falling into place.

I ran and threw myself onto my dad.

"I'm going to Spain! I'M GOING TO SPAIN!"

I pranced around the living room, forgetting the piercing hangover I had groggily nursed for the entirety of that day.

I was being validated.

I was starting a new chapter.

But wait.

What would I tell Trevor?

Would Trevor still want to be with me if I went to Spain?

I allowed this habitual proclivity to focus on the negative assume control. Worry and doubt blew in, slightly darkening the high that was introducing me to the beginning of the rest of my life.

All of a sudden, Trevor meant so much to me without any verifiable reason. It was a response without rationalization. It was the incarnation of The Black Keys' lyrics.

But everybody knows that a broken heart is blind.

I drove down to San Diego for our lunch meeting at a café off campus.

We sat across from one another as he explained how busy he was this quarter with his new role in a production, teaching, and his responsibilities as a grad student. As he said this, I was mentally frolicking through my imagination, too mesmerized by his voluntary presence in my real life to fully absorb the content of his message.

We took a walk around the cove, conversing in brief spurts distinctly delineated by uncomfortable silences. We would behold the nondescript patch of grass in front of us, suffering through the stinging chill of the spring air until someone broke the barrier with sound, propelling us forward again.

What felt like a glacial shuffle between two senile citizens eventually gave way to us utilizing our youth to sit down upon a patch of grass near an idle gang of seagulls.

"Com'ere, Fred!"

Trevor was calling one of the seagulls over as you would a trained dog.

"I'm sorry—did you just call that bird, *Fred?*"

"Yeah. Why?"

"There are two seagulls that always sit on the balcony at work, and we nicknamed them Fred and Wilma. It's weird that you would randomly call a seagull *Fred.*"

He just smiled.

Considering the lack of material covered on our first date, once in the parking lot, I finally divulged my volatile news.

"So, I just found out that I'm going to Spain in September."

"No way!"

"Yeah. I'll actually be moving there to teach English for a year."

"That's awesome." He became lost in his own thoughts. "I loved backpacking through Europe."

"When did you do that?"

"After I graduated from undergrad. Being alone like that definitely changes how you see things."

That is precisely what encapsulated the disconnect between Trevor and me.

All the things he had done that I hadn't.

> *I wanted him to embrace me in my naiveté, deconstructing the minute details of his life, forgetting the passage of time, tying knots with the ribbons of our souls.*

But my disappointment in his unmatched willingness to map out his private thoughts for me during our first casual encounter was but a scratch from brushing up against a jagged branch. I filled the drive back to Orange County with images of the next time we would hang out when the impediments to my forging a connection with someone an hour away came into view. This obviously meant that in order to have more time to spend together I needed to quit my job.

A fter one agonizing week apart, I drove back down to meet Trevor for dinner.

I was effusively giddy to be with him, clashing with his somber mood, when about halfway through dinner, he interrupted my peppy rant.

"This isn't going to go anywhere."

I didn't necessarily believe him.

"Why do you say that?"

"Just, you shouldn't get too close to me."

I heard him, and I am sure I responded appropriately, but, internally, I disregarded what he had said as a fact of our relationship.

I had spent so much time solely focused on grinding to climb up the ladder of success that I no longer saw the value in doing it alone. My pursuit of stability had sucked my soul dry, and I assumed other people must feel the same way. Craving the companionship of another to lessen the blow of the loneliness that accompanies the momentary breath of waking hours left over between sleep and real-life responsibilities.

Maybe he just didn't have enough time to truly feel his loneliness. Or maybe I was foolishly blind.

I didn't hear from him for a week until I finally gave in and called him, leaving a voicemail concerning the prospect of a next date. He called me back the next day, explaining his crazy rehearsal schedule, but insisted that I come to opening night of his play a few weeks later.

Done.

S cout and I attended the preview of Trevor's play together as two of the ten people in the auditorium.

Uncertain of what relationship level we were on, Scout and I headed back to his place after it was over, and I texted Trevor inviting him to hang out whenever he was done.

Trevor: *Okay. Cool. Just finishing up with notes.*

I took his shift in amenability to not only see me but to hang out with my friends as an early sign of progress.

Trevor glided through the epitome of an undergrad's living quarters, unaffected by the assortment of unclaimed panties that hung from the chandelier complementing the various posters of girls posing in swimsuits. He sat down on the worn-out cushions around the tarnished coffee table to partake in some of Scout's stash before suggesting our departure for his apartment.

M otivational post-it notes adorned his side of the bathroom mirror.

He had authorized a level-five privacy breach, presenting his room to me.

Pictures pinned to his bulletin board. The assortment of books on the nightstand. The strategically placed bonsai tree in front of the only window in his cozy quarters.

I spent an unknown amount of time lingering before I realized that he wasn't by my side, admiring my admiration of him.

I moseyed into the living room, where the hypnotic sounds of Bon Iver accompanied the flickering dance of burning tea candles bordering the perimeter of the space.

My heart amplified.

We sipped on wine, naturally drifting in and out of conversation when Trevor intently grabbed my hand.

"Do you want to watch the stars?"

He led me back into his bedroom and turned off the lights. Glow-in-the-dark stars illuminated the ceiling above his bed.

It was corny, but I was smitten.

We laid on his comforter, staring at the ceiling, a physical bubble separating us. I wanted him to kiss me, but he was stiff as a board.

"Trevor?"

"Yeah?"

"Will you kiss me?"

A palpable pause.

"Sure."

The pressure release shot my heart through the plastic cut outs on his ceiling.

The permanent fixture of clouds of doom were dissipating. My fingertips ran across the cool clay on the other side.

Destiny.

While he went to class and taught during the day, I took advantage of my free time to lay on the beach, write, and go to yoga, inhabiting this never-before-seen relaxed version of myself.

The only hiccup was that when I slept over at his place, I couldn't sleep. I wanted to take in every moment for fear that it was going to vanish before I had gotten my fill. The anxiety over losing this person that I longed to be with haunted my subconscious, further tainting my rose-colored glasses.

Happiness cloaked my obsession.

Perspective

My parents were the original architects of my perspective. Interactions with them—revealing their habits, behaviors, mannerisms, and worldviews—could not be avoided. By default, they were my examples of adulthood, responsibility, love, trust, and marriage. But these frames of reference, braced by rusted nails, shattered when I moved back home.

It wasn't the glass breaking that made me realize something wasn't aligning nor was it my attempt to pick up all the broken pieces with the goal of putting them back together again. It was finding photos tucked behind the only images I had ever seen displayed in the frames that brought all the relevant aspects of life that we had never discussed into view.

Years into the future, I will be writing at Intelligentsia when a man will tap me on the shoulder, interrupting my train of thought.

"Hey. That is one of the old MacBooks, right?"

"I think so."

"They don't make them like they used to, huh?"

"I guess not."

I will slightly pause. His irrelevant comments lack a clear

direction.

"I just got back from a conference in Mexico. I am a holistic doctor and I was giving a lecture there... Let me show you something."

He will put his bag down, capturing my attention by scanning my body with certain eyes. His arbitrary insertion into my world will paralyze me.

"Put your feet on the ground."

I will inch my feet from the barstool railing onto the floor and turn to face him.

"Now create a triangle between your feet and the top of your heart."

His command will not be abrasive or unwelcomed and although weird, I am a supporter of the weird and always invite it to play out as it may.

"Now close your eyes and breathe into that space." He will wait a few beats before asking, "How does that feel?"

I will begin to form a response.

"No. Don't think about it. Just feel it."

I will sit there with my eyes closed for a few more breaths before opening them again to his shining face, patiently smiling. He will look deep into my eyes, engaging my soul, and will illuminate it with his words.

"The only thing that separates us from one another is our experiences."

He will write his name—Adam—and phone number down in the cover of my notebook before leaving just as surreptitiously as he had appeared.

I will not be able to process whatever had just elapsed save the correlation between his name and the biblical father of humanity.

I will pack up my things, operating on automatic, and walk outside past the line, but he will not be waiting for coffee.

I will look right and then left down Abbot Kinney before I see him about fifteen paces ahead, walking with firm intention, never looking back.

H is words will solidify the feelings surrounding my past.

Our experiences inform our perspectives. Therefore, our perspectives are what separate us from one another.

Neither my parents' perspectives nor feelings towards the world will ever fully be the same as mine because the way they experience life is uniquely their own. Teaching me about the world is different from telling me the way that it is and I had confused the two.

I had wanted someone to give me a detailed road map rather than glossing over the large potholes that riddle the road of adulthood. I was frustrated by adults' withholding of information, conveniently forgetting to mention the terrestrial tests we all must endure.

No one had explained the retrospective process that comes with being alive. That only once we get to the other side of an obstacle (or joy) can we derive meaning. And, more importantly, only we can derive the meaning of our lives for ourselves.

There is not any one answer, route, or journey. Every detail is uniquely tailored to our souls, fueled by our pursuit of truth; our reason for being here; the meaning of life.

His presence will offer the reason why my parents could not warn me of the challenges I would encounter.

Their experiences have been different because what they are here to learn is inherently different.

Bringing me to the catch-22 of the parent-child relationship.

We rely upon the perspectives of others whom we trust when we are growing up because we lack the experience necessary to formulate our own. Although these lessons that our elders have derived from their own lives are a part of our journeys, they cannot save us from learning the lessons necessary to our own personal journeys.

In other words, we are destined to get lost.

Expectations

The next memorable evening that Trevor and I shared, we planned on going downtown for dinner at my favorite restaurant.

I got ready at my parents' house, applying makeup—a rarity—complemented by a flashy outfit, eager to be seen in public as a couple. But when Trevor picked me up at my car, he did not carry half the excitement I did. A comparison easily represented by showing up in the same jeans and t-shirt he had been wearing all day.

I expected a lot out of Trevor.

There were several voids I expected him to fill that I did not yet know how to fill for myself. But neither he nor I acknowledged these shortcomings. For the sake of comfort, it was easier for me to overlook our incompatibilities by swallowing my expectations, chasing them with hope.

Hope that he would figure it out.

Hope that he cared enough to figure it out.

Hope that it would change.

I waited as long as I could for him to be the one that coaxed me out of my childish sulk, but the viscosity floating this boat of our relationship could not be thinned without a flame. And it was an unseasonably cold spring.

Almost every discussion at dinner ended in an argument, giving more time than customary to chew, bringing our first romantic meal together to an abrupt close. The check came—which we split— and I was preparing myself for the tense car ride back to the school campus I never wanted to see again.

Hope that he would figure it out.

Hope that he cared enough to figure it out.

Hope that it would change.

He knew I had made a reservation for post-dinner libations at a speakeasy, but I still hadn't learned how not to stab myself with a shard of my broken expectations. So I asked the question I already knew the answer to—"Do you still want to go to Prohibition?"— when he said, "Sure."

We proceeded to the disguised law office across the street and rang the doorbell.

A bouncer emerged after a good minute of us trying to decide how long we should wait for something to happen. He checked us in and closed the door. I wasn't familiar with the protocol—waiting for undesignated periods of time—wishing that something would finally work out right and exceed our lackadaisical anticipation. He reappeared again, unclipped the rope, and motioned for us to follow him inside.

We descended a dim staircase into a red-hued room, evoking 1920s nostalgia: the paradox of hushed activities stowed underground yet enlivened by the brass voice of a live jazz band.

Trevor propped himself against the bar, waiting for our flapper-themed bartenders to finish crafting our artisanal cocktails, while I sat at a nearby booth, willing the funky vibes to permeate and alter my mood. Trevor returned, setting down our drinks without taking a seat. He grabbed my hand, dragging me onto the dance floor in the center of the room.

He pulled my body into his, confidently leading us through the steps so I didn't have to think. Stevie Wonder's iconic "Isn't She Lovely" aroused levitation, my imagination aiming a spotlight on our embrace. There was no such thing as stable ground; but, as long as he eventually came around to hold me up, it was a gesture that neutralized an inordinate amount of negatives combined.

W ho I was now would never recognize the me from just a few hours ago in the very same spot in his car.

The silence between us was the most relaxed it had ever been, provoking me to divulge things I would normally never say.

"I told my eighty-nine-year-old grandmother about you."

He didn't respond, but it didn't matter. I was on a high.

"Do you still talk to your grandparents?"

All I knew was that he wore his grandfather's dog tags.

"Well, my grandmother passed just a few years back."

The hesitation in his voice; the wound was still fresh.

"That must be hard. What do you remember most about her?"

He took this in.

"She used to stroke the inside of my arm—"

Lost in memory, he trailed off.

I couldn't help but focus on how that related to me. I waited a second before confirming.

"I do that to you."

"I know."

That was the first and only night we made love in a way that was present. Both of us abandoning whatever was going on in our minds or our hearts that had previously held us back from being fully engaged with one another.

Or it could have been the effects of a higher BAC than usual.

Regardless, it was the only night I ever slept soundly by his side.

The next morning, while we were out to breakfast, it was clear that the pendulum had swung back into its natural territory.

Trevor had traded his transient interest back for his normal ways of being: lost in thought.

We sat on a cliff overlooking the beach, the PCH train tracks eight feet from our backs. Our legs dangled off the dusty edge, and he had hardly spoken. I was gazing into the Pacific Ocean, longing to know what he was thinking about when I budged.

"What's up?"

"I have a lot of stuff going on."

I was finally allowing myself to accept that something was off. Tension had been established during our first dinner together, building up to the current level of dissonance too palpable to suppress.

We got back into his car so he could drive me to my car before class. But before I could put on my seatbelt, he said, "I can't do this."

"What do you mean?"

He proceeded to explain that not only was it not going to work, but it clearly wasn't working.

"I think you're great, but we shouldn't keep doing this anymore."

I did not know what to do. I was listening but I couldn't believe him.

Why would he do all the things he had done just to tell me that he couldn't see me anymore?

I ugly cried the entire hour-long drive back to Orange County. This was beyond rejection. My expectations had exploded.

My envisioned prince had carried me on his back, the damsel in distress I was, to the top of the mountain, just to drop me from said pinnacle and walk away unscathed as I tumbled back into the unknown.

I wanted him to feel all the pain I had been harboring for the past two and a half years. I wanted it to resonate with him so we could heal our pain together. And, as I free fell, I had the rudest awakening.

We did not want the same things.

I thought I could force him to change his mind by overpowering him with the strength of my passion. I knew it was impossible to make someone feel the same way as me, but my mind and my heart could not agree over how to navigate reality while honoring my feelings.

I was still throwing myself full-heartedly into endeavors that came my way, only to be left bruised and battered by these experiences. I did not know how to protect myself from people or obstacles disguised as opportunities because I did not want to be numb to what was taking place in my life.

Everyone seemed to be walking around with hidden pain. Pain they didn't want to expose and covered up, like Trevor had with the conventional avoidance of actually putting himself out there and talking about what he felt.

It confused me.

> *How could all the ways I wanted life to happen be consistently inconsistent with the situations that actually played out in reality?*

I needed a new distraction.

I needed to flee and abandon all visible triggers of pain.

I called Theresa, my college roommate from junior year, who was living in San Francisco to see if I could live with her for a couple of months over the summer.

"Uh, duh."

I flew up there a week later, relishing in the reunion with someone who could always bring out my weird side and lived in the name of having fun.

Since Theresa worked during the day, I had ample time that needed filling.

So I called Regina.

Originally from NorCal, she was home for the summer, and we embarked upon one of our traditional nature walks through Marin County.

The trail was ripe with conversation, and we were on the lookout for a place to perch and extend our necks towards the sun like lizards seeking heat. But I struggled to find the warmth in the light, the reassurance of happiness delivered by the sun, and she spotted it.

"What's wrong?"

It was the permission I had been seeking to open the floodgates. To cry because Trevor told me to leave. To cry because my parents were still unhappy and struggling. To cry because all of this affected me, and I did not know what to do, how to cope, or who could help me dig through this avalanche of pain.

"I don't know how to smile anymore. Every time someone passes me in the street and smiles, I put my head down because I want to cry. I can feel how big the gaping hole in my heart is, and I don't know what to do."

"You need to go home."

It was so simple yet so fear-inducing.

After three years, I was finally addressing that **something was wrong with me.** I did not feel whole and, moreover, did not know how to become whole again.

I texted my mom notifying her that I had booked a flight back to Orange County before informing Theresa of the same later that night. It took everything in me to hold it together in the presence of one of my friends who had never been the shoulder to cry on but, rather, the person who made me pee my pants from laughter. And, for the first time in the four years that we had been friends, Theresa fell serious.

"I am so sorry," she said as tears filled her eyes, "I know **exactly** how that feels."

She had never offered her deepest strife to me during the year we lived together, nor would I have ever suspected that she had been through her own version of identity loss. But somehow my admission had given her permission to share the pain she had carried throughout high school, events catalyzed by the loss of her mother. We sat on the couch hugging one another, strengthening the bond of a long-distance friendship that we would have to continue to maintain from afar.

It took the blunt honesty of two friends to catalyze the courage needed to release the hurt I had locked away.

I had been so consumed with attaining gratification from tangible undertakings—school, work, and the pursuit of intimate relations—that I had never stopped to process the subsequent feelings attached to each failure, heartache, or disappointment. This backlog of tenderness had compiled into layers and hardened into a remote island of pain. An island of my own making. A product of my habitual reaction to flee. I faced the discomfort and sat in my parents' backyard for the two and a half months leading up to my momentous departure undisturbed.

Every couple of days, a new realization would pinch my soul, causing me to transition through a spectrum of emotions—grief, anger, self-admonishment, pity, frustration, and mourning—before my heart would scab over and shut down until I had enough strength to reboot and feel again.

In between purges, I wrote and researched, educating myself on the lives of authors who had led tragic existences themselves.

I felt a kinship to them.

I felt that, if anything, this pain was for solidifying that one part of my identity as a writer.

But, simultaneously, I couldn't focus on the prospects of being a writer because I was dealing with every other facet of my identity having become unrecognizable to the point of isolation.

I did not know who I was, who I was becoming, or who I wanted to be.

Nor could I understand how my parents did not acknowledge

this withdrawal in me.

As a cognitive science professor, my mother was someone I assumed would understand and encourage me to seek therapy. But a lack of money still haunted her, and she had become as unrecognizable to me as I had become to myself.

She was always stressed and uptight. Laughter did not come easily as it once had. When I told her that I needed to talk to someone about how I was feeling, her taking offense should not have come as a surprise.

"Why?"

"Because I don't feel well. There's something wrong with me."

"It's probably your birth control."

"Mom. **I'm depressed.**"

I choked back tears. I wanted her to hear my words without getting defensive over her interpretation of how these words were a reflection of her as a mother.

"Well, we can't afford for you to see anyone right now."

Her words echoed through my core, scraping me with her subconscious fixation over money.

She had not yet learned that we were being asked to emotionally and mentally adapt to these financial circumstances that were beyond our control.

But, clearly, I could not say this to her. She didn't even respect the objectivity of my feelings.

The most painful part of these exchanges was that all I wanted was my mom to take care of me. But, to her, without access to money, what else could she give me that would make me feel better besides her empathy, her relinquishment of denial, or an apology?

Since we could not afford an outside provider, I was sent to a free therapy circle hosted by a local wellness clinic.

Every hair follicle along my body constricted as I sat in an unlit conference room of a medical building, eyes closed, while fountain water trickled through the speakers of a boom box for sixty minutes.

I felt above sharing this sterile environment with strangers, who were also searching for a way to "manage" their existence. I was self-evidently more in tune than them: a yoga practitioner, familiar with breathwork, negotiating her pain as a writer's path to one's greatest life works.

Each day leading up to Spain manifested my unresolved frustration in ways such as this, forcing me to confront my consistent pattern of victimized thinking: *never getting what I want when I seemingly think I need it most.*

Although, in one sense, I knew that taking time to process my feelings for myself was valuable, my default settings would regularly malfunction, suggesting the benefits of someone else doing it for me.

A professional, my parents, Trevor, god...

Anyone to heal my pain other than me.

PART TWO:
SPAIN

The Journey

I woke up early to attend what would be my last yoga class for the next year of my life.

With the precise state I had lamented for the whole of summer—isolation—mere moments out of reach, I stopped for an açai bowl on the way home, indulging in the epitome of trendy SoCal food during a private goodbye to the solitude that would no longer be. It was all supposed to be bittersweet. It was all supposed to feel heavy and meaningful. But it wasn't until I returned home to find my entire family—my grandma, dad, mom, and brother—waiting for me outside to share a final breakfast feast together that I realized how all these profound moments were rolling past me like tumbleweeds.

"Why didn't you text me?" I accused my mother as I took a seat on the patio where I had spent the last two months alone.

"We wanted to surprise you."

My family picked at their plates, none of us knowing exactly what to say.

"Don't you want to eat?"

"I had an açai bowl after yoga."

My brother hid his smirk from her view.

He knew.

He could feel her suppression and redirection of swallowed

emotions into preparing a fancy breakfast reserved only for Christmas morning, too.

That is why we spent the two-and-a-half-hour drive to LAX in the backseat of the only car on the 405 freeway not listening to the radio, texting one another.

Bro: *She's handling this really well.*

Me: *I wonder if she'll ever talk again.*

Bro: *Probably not til you get back.*

The first hour of my parents' four-hour cushion was spent parking at the wrong terminal, wandering around until we found a sky attendant informed enough to direct us toward our designated point of departure. We extended the unnecessary detour by opting to walk (rather than drive) through the concrete death trap of LAX. I was ready to realize the imminence of my trip and send them and their novice antics on their way, but the airline kiosk still had thirty minutes before it opened. So the four of us idly huddled around the single large suitcase I was checking. My mom looked like someone had just announced her physical description alongside her diagnosis of anal polyps over the loudspeaker while my father inhabited the opposite realm of aloofness, looking off into the distance wearing a stupid grin.

In time-lapse mode, more people arrived, standing behind us in line, saying their goodbyes, until an airline employee finally signaled me to the desk. The fixture of my suitcase bumped along the conveyor belt, and a long overdue boarding pass was placed in the palm of my hand.

My mom grabbed my waist, pulling her body into my chest. "Mom, it's going to be fine."

She was quietly sobbing, pulling a tissue out of her purse, as I moved to hug my dad.

"Have fun, baby."

I embraced my sixteen-year-old brother last.

"Love you."

As soon as we let go, my mom was back again, pushing a stack of cards into my hand.

"Read these on the plane."

Her recoil was faster this time, moving back to stand by my dad, aware that if she came toward me again she might never let go.

But I couldn't help smiling.

It was happening.

A member of airport personnel requested my boarding pass to board the escalator. I only looked back to wave once.

I found a spot in the food court.

"Do You Believe in Magic?" by the Lovin' Spoonful played over the loudspeaker.

Without thinking, I broke the seal on my first journal for this trip, inspiring a stream of aspirations mixed with instructions.

> *Go with the flow.*

> *Make new friends.*

> *Gain fluency in Spanish.*

> *Relinquish expectations.*

> *Visit as many places as possible.*

And the most important one.

> *Say 'yes' to everything.*

I arrived in Seville after sleeplessly traveling for twenty-one hours. My ceremonious steps into my final destination led me to the baggage claim, where fluorescent lights buzzed across neglected walls of formerly white paint. Every minute that passed waiting for my bag to appear felt like five. My vivid daydreams of exploring new frontiers had been strangled by exhaustion.

I was putting the pieces together as I noticed them, recognizing the taxi line as my next stop when I walked outside. Once it came to my turn to communicate with the toothless conductor, linguistic reinforcements thankfully kicked in. They collected as many salvageable Spanish sentence constructions from high school as they could to clumsily convey the address before I slid into the backseat.

The heat at eight o'clock at night. The leather sticking to the backs of my thighs. The tobacco fumes from the ashtray wafting into the backseat. The murky breeze from the necessary open window.

We drove through a shabby urban landscape of rundown freeways, abandoned warehouses along the side of the road, gas stations, and faded billboards. After twenty minutes, we arrived at a hotel embedded within a grove of silver-faced high rises. I thanked the man as he released my bag, turning to enter the prosaic building, convincing myself that everything would look different—authentically Spanish—once I had slept.

The program coordinator was pacing with her clipboard in the lobby, impatiently awaiting the last arrival: me.

"Put your things in room 307. Dinner is already in progress."

I took the claustrophobic lift to find two sets of luggage already present.

So I guess I am staying in a room with only two beds and two other strangers...?

Glad I got a heads up.

Dinner was taking place in a typical hotel ballroom with round banquet tables dressed in scratchy white linen. Each table displayed a small piece of cardstock labeled with a different region of Spain. I scanned the ten fully occupied tables, boisterous with Americanism, for *Andalucía*. I approached my region's group without any acknowledgment from the ten Americans fixated on the boy mid-explanation.

They were playing icebreakers.

My body tensed in protest of forced participation. I just wanted to rest, alone, and wake up re-energized to discover the Spain of my dreams.

I passively listened to everyone talk about "back home," validating my personal mandate of not spending time with other Americans because no one cared about cremating their American identity as much as me.

On our third night, our TEACH tour guides led us into the picturesque foyer of an antiquated Spanish house.
Silhouetted by original Roman columns was a stage.
The lights dimmed.

I had no frame of reference for the historical dance of the *flamenco* beyond Federico García Lorca's explanation of the *duende*.

**Duende: a mysterious power which everyone senses
and no philosopher explains.**

It is said that what determined whether *flamenco* was a performance or a transcendental experience was the presence of the *duende* in the performers. But, for me, this explanation validated something unrelated. This Spanish writer from the early 1900s was confirming that he had also witnessed the same greater power that drew me to people, places, and things no one could explain, and that no one—besides myself—had seemed to notice.

The costumed dancers emerged to the guitarist's feathered pluck of *flamenco* strings. A courtship of anguished dress flapping and *machisto* toe stomping. The bellowing cries of a male singer, tucked into the shadows of the background, who kept beat with his hands. The sensory ignition of his voice alchemized foreign words into universal feeling. The male dancer exited the stage, leaving the woman breathless and despondent in the spotlight. Her loaded silence ruptured into a crescendo of heel clapping, woefully casting out her loneliness, dancing her way through pain, indifferent to the figurative blood she trailed across the stage. She exited, the stains of her pain glistening on the stage as he entered from the other side, his internal process made manifest by his thunderous steps. He was consumed by her existence yet fighting this irrational temptation to be bound to a single life form for the remainder of his waking days. But, by the end of his catharsis, the stage was bare. Her blood had transfused through the soles of his feet.

El cantante filled the gap in movement with a visceral solo of solidifying sound. The man and woman took the stage for the final time, entering from opposite sides to reunite center stage. They were not dancing in contention like before nor in ceremony to convey a fairytale ending. Rather, the erratic alternation of their steps—from violent to tender—symbolized their journey to mutual acceptance of this fact of life.

Pain exists both with and without love.

A message I blocked from comprehension.

I refused to accept the pain of partnership.

I looked to art for hope, not torture. Not to confirm my past. Life was not going to be like that for me anymore. Wincing through anguish, calling upon the duende to save me from myself, from the harsh truths of reality, from the agony born from loving something you cannot have.

Art penetrated my vulnerable psyche, exposing wounds faultily bandaged with hope.

Spain was nothing like I thought it would be.

After three days of hotel accommodations, we were each placed in different neighborhoods throughout the city with a local family.

During our homestays, we would attend language classes in the mornings, leaving the remainder of the day open to do as we pleased. My homestay household was composed of a married couple—Maria and Jakal—and Jakal's cousin. Jakal's cousin was from Andorra and did not speak Spanish or English, while Jakal was from Morocco, and Maria was a native *Sevillana*. I felt welcomed into their home but mostly grateful that I had been put into an environment where no one spoke English.

During my first afternoon there, I was nursing a severe hangover contracted from too much *fiesta* from the night prior. (Two weeks would have been a long-ass time to adhere to principle and avoid making any friends in the program because they were American. I wasn't *that* extreme).

After exchanging kisses on both cheeks with each family member, and completing a tour through every room of my temporary home, I politely retired to my private quarters for a *siesta*.

Seville is sweltering during the summer, forcing its inhabitants to spend the afternoons of high sun inside (hence the Spanish *siesta*). Despite the fan in my room and the open window, I was sweating so much that I was dissolving into the bed. I assumed that since the living room was larger, it probably had more aeration, so I could relax in there and spend some time with the family instead. I opened the doors to the salon to find Maria and Jakal's cousin dressed in robes, on their knees, bowing forward toward the open window. I stood there, not knowing what to do before realizing that it would be more appropriate to close the door rather than stare at their synchronized continuation of prayer.

Why wouldn't they tell me that they were going to pray?

I returned to my room and decided to use the heat to my advantage—as a sleeping pill—ignoring the side effects of sweat, passing out in all my glory.

To my surprise, no one brought up my ritual interruption at dinner that night. In fact, no one was engaging with each other at all. The TV screen was less than a foot away from the dinner table, capturing their attention between bites. A short-lived engagement at that. It only took them about five minutes to crook their necks over bowls of unrecognizable mush—a lentil concoction containing at least twenty different spices—and finish their meals. Having only lightly touched my mush, I politely excused myself.

Refuge had yet to be found.

A couple days of language classes magnified another shortcoming. My Spanish speaking abilities.

I was in desperate need of concentrated conversation. So when I returned home for lunch, I was invigorated to find everyone present with whom I could practice. However, once at the table, they assumed their habitual stance: inhaling their food with eyes glued to the screen. I was actively thinking of any way to generate conversation outside whatever indeterminable topic was featured on the news.

At the end of every meal in Spain, there is fruit available on the table to eat. They have this efficient way of peeling fruit in one swift motion that I dared not replicate. So I reached into the bowl to retrieve an orange and asked Jakal to peel it for me.

"Me la pelas?"

Jakal looked at me, mouth agape, before breaking into uncontrollable laughter. His eyes filled with tears, and he was unable to speak. I repeated myself, which only made him laugh harder, and, by this point, Maria had joined in with him. The cousin just shrugged when I looked to her for an explanation before looking back at Maria. She gathered herself to a point before giggling while gesturing her hand in the "jerking off" position.

The homestay cuisine did not improve, so I often ate out with my friends instead.

On this particular night, we were going to take the bus across the bridge to an Irish pub to watch an NFL game. I told Jakal of my evening plans as I was walking out the door, and he stopped me.

"Wait."

Jakal scuttled down the corridor, returning moments later with a man's leather crossbody purse.

(The economic recession was still in full effect in Europe [referred to as *la crisis* in Spain]. Theft had risen and our Spanish guides were worried about foreigners, especially women, being more susceptible to this social danger).

Although I was not opposed to being gifted this androgynous hobbit satchel, I also wanted to learn how to fit in on my own.

I reeked of contradictions.

I wanted people to help me but on my own terms, in the way I thought I needed.

He handed me his bus card for the fare, placing his other hand on my shoulder.

"Be safe."

Three friends and I stood on the street corner. Tom, the eldest and most proficient speaker, was reading the posted schedule as a bus rolled to a stop on the opposite side of the street.

He calmly gazed up at the sound of an engine disengaging before realizing, "That's our bus! Go!"

We were not near a crosswalk, and, for some reason, when another person yells *Go!*, people are quick to oblige.

We ran across the street, barely clearing the quickly approaching cars, as the bus kicked into gear. Tom hit the side of the bus.

"¡Espera!"

The bus driver reluctantly stopped, not withholding his disapproval. The doors parted to let us in. His stern glare grew in severity with each person that paid and passed.

I was the last one in line, and by the time it was my turn, the bus

driver impatiently closed the doors on my tail and began to drive.
Considering the bus driver's attitude, I was examining the situation
for clues on how to use this bus card. My brain impulsively
interpreted the most accessible slot as a credit card slot, so I pushed
the bus card into it. But it wouldn't slide in and out.

It had gotten stuck—no, jammed.

I was sweating, tugging on what was left of it, when the bus
driver finally glanced over to see what was taking me so long. He
looked as if I was strangling his cat right in front of him, emoting in
Spanish and groaning before stopping the bus in the middle of the
street. He got out of his contained shell to open the ticket feeder;
the device I had mistook as the card reader. He retrieved my card
and swiped it against a sensor on the pole when you first walk in,
restraining himself from spitting on me.

As I turned to face the back of the bus, every Spanish passenger's
expression informed me that I had interrupted their normally
smooth commute. A harsh welcome softened by the laughter of
my American companions. I took my seat, laughing alongside
them, withholding that this was my first time ever boarding a
metropolitan bus.

The next day, all members of my homestay were present at lunch
again.

Jakal and I were conversing when he casually mentioned that he
spoke seven languages. I was intrigued as to why he wasn't utilizing
this skill in a more professional capacity (he was a cab driver).

"How do you know so many languages?"

"I used to work in a hotel."

Okay, now we were getting somewhere.

"Jakal! I used to work in a hotel, too! What did you do?"

He withheld a response, lowering his gaze down toward his
plate. Usually when this happened, I assumed someone couldn't
understand my broken accent or I had incorrectly formed my

sentence, so I repeated myself.

"I worked at the front desk of a hotel. What did you do?"

Again, no response.

Finally, from the opposite end of the table, Maria chimed in.

"He used to like... the ladies..."

Whoosh.

Her sentence flew over my head.

"*¿Comó?*"

She repeated herself, emphasizing the use of her eyebrows.

"He used to like (*eyebrow raise, eyebrow raise*) the ladies (*wink, wink*)."

I lost all control of my reactionary functions as I realized that Jakal used to be a gigolo. Not only that, **they were telling me that he was a retired gigolo.** And his current wife was the one responsible for revealing such information.

She laughed as I translated her words in my head. Jakal raised his glance to make eye contact with me, confirming the validity of this claim as he bashfully shrugged.

The other participants in the program had homestays with Spanish moms requesting to be called *señora*, who would make them delectable authentic meals, such as Spanish *tortilla* and *gazpacho*.

Two of my friends' *señora* had gotten so hot one afternoon that she walked around the house without a blouse on, as if my friends were a part of her family. This same *señora* and her husband also took these friends out to *discotecas* and *flamenco* clubs, relinquishing the role of responsible adult to her homestay visitors, who would have to persuade her that two a.m. meant it was time to go home.

Meanwhile, in my neck of the foreign woods, my normal bodily functions were not performing as they should.

It had been ten days... ten days!

And I woke up with piercing pains in my abdomen.

Was it the food? Was it the water? Or was it just that I had yet to move a bowel?

131

I Skyped my dad, lying in bed, almost in tears.

"What's up?"

"Dad. I can't poop."

He combusted with laughter as he usually did when I had something serious to talk to him about.

"Dad! Stop! What am I gonna do?!"

I was wincing through the pain.

"You need to take a laxative."

"I don't know how to say that in Spanish. What am I supposed to do? Just tell them I can't poop?"

"I don't think you have a choice. Have you pooped at all?"

I shook my head.

He laughed again. "Good luck!"

Barely able to stand due to severe intestinal cramping, I resembled Quasimodo as I hobbled down the hallway toward the salon to see who might be home, praying it wasn't just the cousin. (I never saw the cousin leave the house. I only saw her go to the market once, but it had been accompanied by Maria on a weekend afternoon. Otherwise, I could find her sweeping, prepping the food I called *slop*, or cleaning).

Luckily, Maria was seated at the table. Her glance was drawn away from the TV set to this horizontal version of myself, and worry took over her face.

"*¿Qué pasa?*"

I paused.

How do I tell her I need to poop?

"Uh... No... *Hacer caca.*"

"*Oh! Oh, no! ¡Qué mala, qué mala!*"

Without further questioning, she gathered her things.

"I am going to the pharmacy. *No te preocupes.*"

It wasn't long before she returned, unveiling the box from the universal white pharmacy bag. But it was not a box of pills.

No.

She had purchased a spouted device.

My eyes widened.

She had bought me **an enema.**

She was shuffling me toward my room, encouraging me to use it in that very moment. I tried to explain to her that I had never used one before, suppressing tears from the mess this had turned into.

She proceeded to lie down on my bed and demonstrate what to do. There was no longer distance between this family and I, even if I had been taking deliberate steps to disassociate myself from them.

This woman was teaching me how to put a spout up my butt.

She left the room, showing me that she would be right outside waiting for me.

Great.

I did what you do, with every step elapsing in slow motion. It took me a couple of attempts before successfully distributing all the juices upstream.

Ashamed and downtrodden, I cracked open the door to find Maria standing there.

"¿Algo ya?"

"No."

I retreated into my room, closing the door before crawling onto the twin cot that I could no longer refer to as my bed since it had become a site of defilement.

I called my mom on Skype, grateful that the silver lining of the situation had an inverse.

They *didn't* speak English.

"Mom, I hate this. This is horrible. They are feeding me horrible food. I can't poop. I hate this. Do you wanna know what happened yesterday?"

I relayed the gigolo story to her, to which she could not stifle a laugh, when all I wanted was someone who could see that this was not living up to any idea that I had for Spain to be.

It was worse than living at home.

With only a few days left at our homestays in Seville, many of us were mentally preparing for the move to our final job sites scattered across Spain.

I had been placed in the south of Spain in a small pueblo called Peñaflor. I tried researching it when I received my placement, but Google only generated one website that pertained to the town. So I emailed the bilingual coordinator of my school—a figure that TEACH strongly encouraged we form a relationship with before our arrival—but she responded a month later without an explanation of the delay and that there was nothing for me to do except show up.

She responded a month later, without an explanation of the delay beyond the fact that she was pregnant. As for everything else, there was nothing for me to do except show up.

So when a girl in the program named Shayna—who had arrived two weeks earlier than me with a separate batch of language ambassadors—reached out to me because she had also been placed in Peñaflor, I felt a gust of luck shift my way.

She had just met with her bilingual coordinator, Ricardo, who offered to pick us both up when we arrived at the train station in Peñaflor later that week. I profusely thanked her, accepting her invitation.

On the final night of my homestay, I returned home from saying goodbye to the other TEACH ambassadors around midnight. Normally, I wandered back home between two and four in the morning, but I had an early train to catch.

I went through my routine of unlocking the door and reaching through the kitchen entryway to switch on the light. The door to the apartment opened into a hallway that extended both straight and right. The kitchen stood to the immediate left. Directly straight led to the salon on the right and the master bedroom across from it on the left. Down the corridor to the right was my room, the cousin's room, our shared bathroom, and a sitting room where Jakal would occasionally host random visitors (men) for tea.

The rest of the apartment was dark when I heard uncustomary rustling from my bedroom corridor. The pitter-patter against the tile grew ever closer until Jakal popped out of the darkness. Scantily clad in his tidy-whiteys, he froze in front of me.

"*Buenas noches, Cee.*"

He scampered down the hallway into the master bedroom and closed the door.

Dismayed and bothered could not encapsulate the apex of weird that had been reached within these four walls. My stay there had ended on the highest note of them all with the revelation that Jakal had sex with his cousin on the nights that Maria was at work.

Get me to my *pueblo*, **now**, please.

The Pueblo

The next morning, Shayna and I boarded the train to our official home.

It was only an hour outside the city, a fact Shayna was supremely grateful for since she was an ardent proponent of Seville.

Her homestay father had been a famous chef, living lavishly in a three-story penthouse above the restaurant the family owned in the popular *barrio* next to the cathedral. The homestay placement gods had also granted her a built-in friendship pool of contemporary Spaniards who worked at the restaurant, gladly integrating her into their microcosm of Spanish nightlife, customs, and colloquialisms.

Shayna spent our first hour together reminiscing about her super sweet Spanish life, leaving me no time to play my violin and explain why I would never be returning to Seville ever again.

Shayna got off the train first, carrying her inflated sense of cultural command, to find Ricardo. I shadowed her, unsure which man in the sparse crowd had obviously been the humane one and invited me along. Shayna, weaving out from behind a large crowd of arrivals, popped into view as she approached a man who threw his hands into the air. He was short with a joyful smile and accelerated presence. He had black spiky hair and a permanent five o'clock shadow and was wearing a pastel blue, wrinkled, cotton polo with jeans. He cheerfully bounced over to me, planting a kiss on each cheek, followed by a vaudevillian handshake.

"It's so nice to have you, Cee!" he exclaimed in a pristine British tone.

"You know English!"

I had yet to encounter a gentleman of his age with such English-speaking proficiency.

"It would seem that way, wouldn't it?"

As well as a cheery sense of humor.

We piled into his miniature European car as he drove us to his residence to meet his family for lunch.

Calles estrechas boasting the standard white stucco buildings with egg yolk golden trim lacked the regal architecture and bustling streets that texturized Seville.

"I have also taken the liberty of setting up nine appointments for apartments today after lunch! Lucia, the girls, and I will all accompany you."

I had resolved to living with Shayna as opposed to trying to find a Spaniard to room with. Shayna had initially shared the same desire as me, but Ricardo had advised her against it since it was nearly impossible to find young, single people living in the *pueblo* alone. And, beyond that, any who would want to share their living quarters with a *guiri* (Spanish for gringo).

Lucia, Ricardo's wife, and Lucia and Camilla, their two daughters, were already at home when we arrived. A paper plate displaying triangles of cheese and freshly cut chorizo sat readily accessible to those of us who hadn't eaten in two weeks.

"Lucia is a teacher, and Lucia and Camilla are both students at Colegio de San José as well, Cee."

I upheld tradition and kissed each cheek of the nine- and eleven-year-old, neither of whom received me with curiosity or vigor but as withdrawn witnesses to the philanthropic antics of their parents, before helping myself to both Shayna's and my appetizers after Shayna said, "I can't eat that. I'm vegan."

Over a homemade lunch of seafood paella, Ricardo carried the conversation in English without pausing to translate for Lucia. "Oh, she's used to it."

We all looked towards Lucia to see if she had been listening. Lost in her own thoughts, she eventually looked up from cutting a piece of squid to see all sets of eyes on her.

Ricardo explained in Spanish why we had been staring.

She giggled nervously while she concentratedly formulated an English sentence in the same way it must have sounded when I spoke Spanish.

"I...," she motioned her right hand side to side to occupy the delay, "understand a little."

It was clear that not only had they done this before, but it was what Ricardo lived for. To vicariously experience his English alter ego through whatever destined reflection landed on this blimp of forgotten land in the countryside of Spain. His authentic interest, on top of every unique strain of the current situation, left me stunned.

Despite my reservations toward Shayna—and her Sevillan coddling that had led to excessive confidence in her Spanish mastery—she had been given the gift of Ricardo. A man so charming that he could convince someone like Shayna of the benefit of saving a seat for someone like me, indirectly extending me the grandest gesture I had received during my first two weeks away from everything I had ever known.

During our apartment tours, we passed through a less than tolerable assortment of places, most of which even our grandmothers would find kitschy.

After eight exhausting appointments, one of which had portraits of cats adorning the walls of every room, we arrived at our last option.

Patricia—also a teacher at Colegio de San José—awaited our arrival outside the door. She was short with rough features and a female mullet. She opened the large brown door into the one-hundred-and-fifty-year-old cottage, moving through the house, speaking a mile a minute as she showed us potential features of interest.

Ricardo quickly intervened.

"The girls just got here. Speak slowly."

Despite Ricardo's helpful warning, Patricia did not become any easier for me to understand. But it didn't matter because Shayna "understood" every detail that was conveyed. She trailed her like a puppy while I drifted in and out of their wake.

This was the first place I could actually envision us living. It held every ounce of rustic charm with two patios—one with a clothesline and another with a table—and creamy white stucco walls decorated with artisanal Spanish tile.

We walked through the kitchen as Patricia demonstrated the outdated process of lighting the gas pilot every time we wanted to use hot water or the stove. There wasn't an oven or a microwave, and the clothesline outside served as the dryer. The sole modern amenity was an eighteen-inch RCA television set from 1990.

After the tour, Ricardo revealed that it would only cost three hundred euros per month to live there.

Shayna and I couldn't believe the bargain. We would only be paying about two hundred USD per month each.

We easily agreed to *la casita antigua*, scheduling a meeting with Patricia at her home to go over the rent contract the following evening.

Patricia's house was slightly bigger than Ricardo's. A fact I only knew because she had given us the customary tour of every room of the house, even taking us into the pantry, where a cured leg of pig—black hoof and bone still intact—laid, supported by a wooden frame, unrefrigerated and ready to sample. Her small stature hoisted the animal remnant onto the counter, grazing an extra-long knife against the exposed layer, slicing fresh *jamón* for me to taste.

My eyes watered from the salty goodness that slipped off the

grisly bone. She poured us each a glass of red wine, leading us
out onto the assembled oasis of hanging plants on her back patio,
insulating us from the omnipotent sun.

We were beginning to settle in when a dusty cowboy swaggered
through the kitchen.

A voice of gravel from smoking cigarettes, the dew of sweat
glistening on his forehead, his disheveled outfit that could be
branded as **careless casual***; the epitome of a man's man was*
standing in the doorway.

It was her husband, Rodrigo.

Separately, they would never have seemed like they went
together. But Patricia's matronly exterior challenged the archetypal
yin to his masculinity.

He spoke in less discernible Spanish than she (a reality I would've
never thought possible) before leaving and returning with multiple
plastic bags full of produce. After the final haul, he grabbed a cold
beer and joined us outside.

We did not discuss matters of business right away. Rather, the
subsequent four hours were spent pausing intermittently for our
delayed translations of their *pueblo* Spanish as they divulged the
intimate details of their idyllic Spanish lives.

Patricia had two brothers, one of whom lived next door to us
and was responsible for managing the family's extensive mass of
farmland. Rodrigo had just returned from said *campo*, bearing gifts
of farm-picked vegetables for Patricia to use in her cooking that
week.

Shayna and I perked up.

"You guys have a farm?!"

Patricia and Rodrigo could not understand why two American
suburban dwellers would be genuinely interested in visiting their
farm, while, simultaneously, we couldn't envision the reality of
owning land like they were describing to grow our own produce.
We set a date for the coming week when they would take us to
their farm, graciously assuring us that we could help ourselves to

whichever crops we wanted to take.

Rodrigo answered our most important question—which cell phone provider was best—and even offered to go with us to mediate the negotiations. They spoke of Córdoba, the next largest neighboring city, and wrote down a list of lively *tapas* bars we should dine at.

Amidst this exchange of our unwarranted enthusiasm for their basic knowledge, I could not stop smiling and saying *gracias* in response to every extension of unearned hospitality. It felt like they were offering so much of themselves when we had nothing to provide besides our linguistically stunted company in return.

"Why do you say *thank you* so much?" Rodrigo spoke emphatically. "If we did not want you here, then you would not be here. Do you understand?"

There was a different philosophy operating here in the pueblo. **Here, life was about spending time with other people.**

They did not have deadlines, excuses, or the impulse to interrupt a conversation to check work emails on their phone. They did not feel obligated to do anything they did not want to. Saying *thank you* to them was not only uncustomary; it was rude.

The thought that people were befriending me and hosting me without knowing who I was or what I could offer them crouched in the back of my mind. I could not help but compare their behavior to the only version of life I knew. A world where people do not have any time and, most especially, would not often make the time to help strangers.

But that was the past.

I was in Peñaflor now, a quaint *pueblo* that offered to suck the Sevillan venom from my veins for no reason beyond the goodness of its heart. Contemplating it further would not have gotten me anywhere because it had already shown me that I was exactly where I was supposed to be.

Teaching English

As I approached my teaching debut, I walked along the outer perimeter of the school playground, which was colored by the universal screams, laughter, and footsteps of children chasing one another. I consciously sheltered my Americanism from view until I reached the front gates, searching for where to go next. Halfway between the gates and the activity of the playground was a door through which parents were alternating entrances and exits. I pushed the door open into a long hallway, where a confident mom charging forth in her heels knocked me out of my stupor. Swallowing my naked nerves, I approached the counter of what appeared to be the secretary's office, squished within a confined space that also functioned as the copy room and mailroom and housed the nurse's cot.

The woman behind the window took notice of me the moment I stepped in line behind the person she was talking to.

"¡La auxiliar nueva!"

She abandoned her conversation, hopping through the door to welcome me instead. She was a geyser spurting jovial gesticulations and unintelligible phrases. I had to wait until she was done to clarify that I did not understand Spanish as quickly as she was speaking it.

"Despacio, despacio."

"Claro."

She made direct eye contact with me, her hands pressing against both of my shoulders as if her physical touch would create an osmotic flow of comprehension.

"I am Jimena."

"I am Cee," I said, delivering my name with a smile.

She tilted her head. "Like, *sí?*"

"*Perfecto.*"

"*Sí... Cee!*"

She laughed at her own joke, grasping my hand to lead me through the teacher's lounge.

Small groups of people of various ages, features, and dress huddled, conversing among themselves.

I desperately willed my bilingual coordinator to appear like a fairy godmother. She did not even have to be as sprightly as Ricardo. I just needed someone to demonstrate how best to maneuver through this maze of Spanish speakers.

Jimena walked me over to a group seated upon the couch, introducing me. Each teacher got up to plant a kiss on both cheeks and tell me their name. Strands of tension loosened with each kiss and sincere embrace, reassuring me that it wasn't the people who were intimidating; it was the cultural divide.

I took a seat at the end of this four-person group on the couch, not knowing whether to interject, listen, or to just sit idly until someone tried talking to me. The man next to me—an older gentleman dressed in a collared shirt with a well-fed face and balding head—nudged my shoulder with his.

"I am new, too," he remarked.

I smiled to disguise my slow translation of his Spanish.

"Miguel Ángel."

"*Gracias, Miguel Ángel.*"

The bell rang, signaling the communal transport of squirrelly children into the next six-hour battle for their attention.

I happened to look toward the doorway just as Lucia was about to head outside. She shuffled over, placing a kiss on each cheek, adoring me like a mother. Having shared my unsuccessful attempt to connect with my bilingual coordinator at lunch the day before,

Lucia intuitively interpreted what I was waiting for.

"I will look for Cristina and tell her you're here, *vale?*"

"*Gracias,*" was all I could reciprocate for the saving grace Lucia had become in the two short days I had known her.

The vacancy of the room left me more uncomfortable than the frenzy before. I returned to the couch, taking in the newly revealed layout of the room. Two 1999 computer desktops sat available for use along the wall next to where I sat, and a disproportionately large wooden table took up the available space in the center of the room.

A young, naturally beautiful woman disrupted my nervous preoccupation. She was not cheerful like Lucia but stoic and focused, directly opposing her gentle features.

"Cee? I am Cristina."

Ahhhh, English.

I had not realized how much I was going to need it until I felt settled.

"Yes. Hello!"

"I have brought you your schedule."

She bypassed the convivial hugs and kisses I had just received from my other coworkers to take a seat across from me, sliding a piece of paper across the table. With the aid of a pencil, highlighter, and ruler she had drawn my schedule by hand. According to this artisanal reference, I would be instructing between ten and fifteen classes each day.

"I don't understand."

"Since there is a *crisis,* you are the only auxiliary we have. You will go to the bilingual classes for both math and science two times each week. And, for the rest of the classes, only for English, just once per week."

The economic recession was not just plaguing America. It was a global catastrophe. Spain was experiencing almost fifty percent documented-worker unemployment. Although it was not affecting everyone directly, it dictated the social atmosphere and no conversation held with an eligible workforce candidate was immune to this hot-button topic.

"It says I am only in each class for fifteen minutes though."

"Yes, because you need to see all classes."

Grades first through sixth each had two classes; one was bilingual and the other wasn't. I would spend two times per week with the bilingual classes and one time per week with the other classes.

"You will have to speak with each teacher to get your lesson plans."

"Okay."

"Now, let's get you to class."

She showed me the two separate buildings, each with two floors and four classrooms per floor. We climbed the stairs in one of the identical buildings, ascending silently to my first door of fate. She pulled it open, revealing Miguel Ángel standing in front of the classroom, readily anticipating our arrival. He patted me on the back, assuring Cristina that he could take it from here.

Although I was grateful for Miguel Ángel's optimism, on this rare occasion, separation from Cristina was the last thing I desired. I turned around to thank her, but the door had already closed.

I followed Miguel Ángel across the front of the room to his desk. He handed me a stack of eight-by-eleven flashcards.

"I thought I was supposed to give a presentation about myself today."

I was piecing together my broken Spanish to explain my confusion.

His expression reflected my concern, but his shrug conveyed that no one had informed him of the computer presentation I had prepared.

"Well, should we try?"

I handed him my USB drive, but there wasn't a projector in the room nor had I brought my computer with me.

"I think we will have to wait until tomorrow. This is our first lesson: body parts."

Before he politely nudged me to the front of the room, he whispered in my ear, "I am not very good at English, so… " and gave me a thumbs up.

It was the only time I would see his class quiet. Twenty sets of six-year-old eyes were fixed on me, having patiently watched their teacher interact with this mysterious figure who had ultimately been released to address them directly.

I held up a flashcard. The image was printed on the front and the word in English was on the back, facing me.

"Nose. Repeat. Nose."

Only one child repeated, quickly covering his mouth with both hands when he realized that no one else had repeated with him.

"No." I spoke more firmly in English. "Repeat."

During our two-day preparation course with the TEACH program director, we had been given specific instructions not to speak to the students in Spanish, for they were not supposed to know that you could understand them. The idea behind this stringent rule was that the kids would be forced to understand what we were saying in English, *not* that they would stop listening because they didn't understand what we were saying.

I repeated myself—"nose"—now using my free pointer finger to touch my nose.

A few kids touched their noses, but the majority looked lost.

Observing my struggle to connect with the kids, Miguel Ángel stepped in toward the middle of the classroom from the back, deliberately touching his nose.

"*Repite,*" he aided.

"Nose," I said.

The kids faintly echoed with Spanish accents, "noooo-sssszzsss."

The next flashcard was mouth. Miguel Ángel said it with me and pointed to his mouth. The kids repeated.

The rest of the day followed a similar pattern of me entering a teacher's domain, meeting them for the first time, and hurriedly being tossed the academic torch of educational responsibility. But the flame gradually dimmed into a flicker, and my hands blistered from burns. The difference between Miguel Ángel and everyone else was his attentive presence. The rest of the teachers regarded my position as a babysitter, burying their faces in their cell phones while I taught. Only one teacher gave specific instructions before checking out, while the remainder only communicated the theme of the lesson for which I employed the help of hangman.

I returned to the teacher's lounge on the prowl for Cristina, but she was not there. Like a lost dog, I roamed the hallway, sniffing her out a few doors down.

"So how was it?"

"Well, I thought during my first week I would be presenting an about-me segment? But I noticed that none of the rooms have projectors."

"I would have to find one for you. Could you do something else?"

My initial impression of this program was a mixture of disorganization, apathy, and doing the best with what they had.

> *The crowded secretary's office that served three different functions, my overloaded schedule, the overarching themes of la crisis...*

"Okay."

"Cee?"

My name floated from the doorway.

A short, sun-kissed man stood there, charged with glee, and repeated himself emphasizing a different meaning.

"*Si!*"

He planted a strong kiss on each cheek.

"I am Luis, the director of the school!"

"Nice to meet you."

The top of his head was even with the highest point of my shoulder. He reached up to rest his hand there, guiding me in a slow stroll down the hallway.

"Ceeee, my nephew needs *clases particulares*. Here is his phone number."

I wasn't in trouble.

He didn't need to verify my identity.

He was helping me with my side-gig. (A side-gig I was also

fundamentally unprepared [unqualified?] for).

He looked up the number in his flip phone, slowing to a stop, as another administrative figure, Eduardo, introduced himself with a kiss on each cheek.

"I was telling her about Alberto," Luis remarked.

"Oh, yes. I know someone who needs *clases particulares* also. I will give you their number tomorrow."

I had envisioned *clases particulares*—unofficial private English lessons—as a grassroots movement that would be difficult to launch in a rural town. But, considering *la crisis'* impact on employment, it made sense. Even people my age were registering for English classes because the places with the greatest chance for employment were Germany and England. The resentment over my birth privilege was being tugged at by the corner. Even though I couldn't fully participate in their language, to the people in the *pueblo*, my native tongue was an asset, not a hindrance.

When I got home, Shayna was not there for me to verbally process my day. So, even though I hated talking on the phone in Spanish (I could not watch someone's mouth while they spoke), I took my roommate's absence as a sign to challenge myself and call Luis' nephew, Alberto.

"Alberto?"

"*Sí?*"

"Hi. I'm the new auxiliary at Colegio de San José. Luis gave me your number."

"Oh, yes. Good afternoon. When can you come by?"

I was not expecting such immediacy. I took a second.

"Uh, now?"

"Great. We live on Juan Carlos."

"Uh..."

"Where do you live?"

"On Plaza de la Libertad."

"Okay. I am right off Calle Nueva near Caixa."

"Uhhh, *no entiendo.*"

"Walk down the street toward the roundabout with the fountain.
Make your first right and take the first left."

We hung up the phone and, in two minutes, I was at his front
door.

I pressed the doorbell on the locked gate. A brief moment later,
a stern woman with long dark brown hair pulled into a braid, an
unfitted dress that reached the floor, and Arabian brown eyes
emerged from the doorway to the house about seven feet away. She
waved me in as I heard the gate buzz open. I pushed it open to walk
up a few steps and cross the landing. The closer I got, it became
clear as to why she had not come to the gate to greet me. She was
restraining her barking German Shepherd, successfully containing
the one-hundred-and-twenty-pound beast by the collar alone.

"Hola. I am Alma."

Such a beautiful name.

She gave me a kiss on each cheek.

Their house was deceiving from where I had waited. The gate
led to the front door, which faced the backyard, where everything
blended together. The patio had not been delineated from the pool
or the pool formally separated from their seemingly endless land of
orange trees.

The interior of the house was reminiscent of an American home.
A detached, two-story home with a grand staircase in the entryway,
spacious bedrooms and bathrooms, warm wood that offset the cold,
white walls accented with Spanish tiles.

I was introduced to their two daughters: Juana, fifteen, and
Cristina, thirteen. They both had dark hair and dark eyes like
their mother, politely smiling back at me without venturing to
interrogate the new girl on the block.

"Do you know Kate?" Alma asked.

"No. Who is that?"

"Oh, she was wonderful. She taught the girls last year."

I just smiled and nodded as she led me into the kitchen, where
Alberto was seated. He rose to give me the customary kisses as

Alma left us to discuss the matters of English alone.

We took our cups of afternoon espresso from the Nespresso machine and sat down across from one another at the majestic, solid-oak table in the kitchen. He was tall and lean with a kind face. He wasn't handsome or homely; only exhaustion painted his face. He slowly explained in English—taking frequent pauses to construct his sentences—how he was the owner of an olive oil company and wanted to learn English to improve his business.

We organized a schedule where I would meet with Cristina and Juana once per week and with him twice. He was fine with the rate, and we planned to meet the next afternoon for our first round of lessons.

Word of my *clases particulares* spread quickly. Within the first two days, I had six clients. I was walking from this apartment to that house, rain or shine, teaching a variety of ages, from a group of two year olds to a pair of sisters—aged seven and ten—to Juana and Cristina. I had a range of lessons to organize for different skill and engagement levels.

And it was fucking hard.

One of the mothers asked me to split the customary one-hour lesson for one person into two slots of thirty-minutes for her seven- and ten-year-old daughters. Each preliminary meeting with prospective students began with an assessment to objectively determine what level I was working with. But even though the sisters were taking English at school, neither of them could spell in English. I opened each of their weekly lessons singing the alphabet with either of them for a few rounds before I released them to sing on their own, but they could never get past letter D without my lead.

They **hated** it.

There were outbursts and shutdowns over my insistence to repeat the alphabet until they got it, which they never did.

Back in America, my move to Spain had represented a fairytale wish come true, especially after the summer I had spent camped out in the perilous swamp of my own making. I romanticized the epitome of the unknown—a foreign land—by filling in the blank with slides from other people's memories via friends' posts of Eurotrips on Facebook. Which is why I would have never imagined all the roadblocks that I had already met within the first month as steps paving my yellow brick road of reward, and that the one consistent theme of my life would serve as the concrete.

The universe shattering every expectation or prediction I held about the future was still a lesson I had yet to learn.

My students' struggles with a foreign language were reflecting such things back to me.

I just wanted Spanish friends to take me under their wings, and massage Spanish into my skin because I wanted a break. I did not want to put extra effort into researching novel ways of stimulating cognitive connections in these kids' brains.

In America, my conscientiousness (my desire [expectation] for [of] results) was considered a remarkable quality, whereas Spain was challenging me to look at this definition differently. Maybe "caring more than others" was not helping anyone; rather, it was placing unrealistic expectations on everyone and everything. Maybe it was time that this aspect of myself that was causing more friction than fluidity be brought to light, so it could be burned off by the omniscience of the southern sun. Maybe Spain was not an exotic escape but another portal through which I must walk in order to shed the outworn layers of my being that not only did not serve me but did not serve my relations with others.

After my session with the two-year-olds, one of the moms asked me if I wanted to hang out with a friend of hers named Mateo.

I had mentioned my desire to meet more people in the *pueblo* after our first session the week prior, and her keen memory of such impressed me.

Shayna and I had no choice but to accept who the *pueblo* was for: families and the elderly. A peer group to do things with was nonexistent. However, life seemed to continually meet Shayna more than halfway.

One of the teachers from Shayna's school, Rafael, his two daughters, and his wife quickly developed a particular fondness for Shayna. She was frequently invited over to receive Spanish cooking training from his wife, after which she would play board games with the girls, then discuss Rafael's teaching methodology in Spanish, most likely over a glass of scotch and a cigar while his pet Golden Retriever laid by the fire.

She spoke so highly of them that I couldn't help but be jealous and want a family to adopt me just the same.

In light of Shayna's Spanish immersion, I eagerly accepted Mateo's number, texting him immediately after my lesson. He was quick to respond, and we planned on meeting for beer in a part of town I had yet to explore later that afternoon.

I had no idea what to expect, unsure of what he looked like or did for a living.

But, on entering the plaza, it would have been difficult to miss the only person sitting at a table at six o'clock in the afternoon. He uncannily resembled Johnny Depp's Captain Sparrow. Baggy and tarnished clothes with small, piercing eyes naturally darkened from a lack of sleep and multiple hoop piercings in each ear. His scraggly goatee rubbed against my cheek as we greeted one another with the standard *besitos*.

He was clearly doing his friend a huge favor by meeting with me because, by the looks of it, we had nothing in common.

We politely asked one another questions as he patiently endured repeating himself so I could translate what he had said. Eventually we got around to him explaining that he was in a band.

"*Muy bien,*" I said.

"No, no, no." He made a face of refusal. "*Es guay, es muy guay.*"

He explained this word by putting up the sign of the horns with his fingers, sticking his tongue out, and screaming, "*Yeah!!!*"

He was erratic and eccentric like this, and what could've been interpreted as embarrassing was exactly what I needed.

Upon parting ways, he invited me to stop by his band's rehearsal later that night, an offer that launched a chain of *yes's* when invited to anything, anywhere, with anyone.

B ack at home, I brought up my new social endeavors, boasting of them to Shayna.

"We should go then."

"Huh?"

"When do they want us to be there?"

It was presumptuous of her to assume that I was inviting her. But as I told her when we should go, I internally agreed that she had been right to include herself when meeting a group of guys in an unfamiliar setting.

R ehearsal was already in progress when we arrived at what we soon realized was an abandoned house.

After waiting for someone to answer the door, Shayna brazenly let herself in. The previously insulated music became our guide to a clearing. Flashlights illuminated remnants of the collapsed ceiling that bordered the edges of the performance area dense with cigarette smoke and dust.

Mateo was propped against a chunk of pillar, puffing a cigarette, looking on as the guys practiced *"Long Train Runnin'."* He motioned us over, intently resuming his focus on the song until it ended a few beats after. The guys were quick to drop character, abandoning their instruments to sheepishly get closer to us. *Besitos* were placed on each cheek while trading names, leaving nothing to do but resume a comfortable distance from their mediocre renderings of American classic rock hits.

Shayna and I nursed *Cruzcampos*, waiting for something extraordinary to strike, but it never did.

To say that it was awkward (the lack of a word for *awkward* or *random* was one of the few minor aspects I did not approve of in the Spanish language; so many of my experiences assumed this tone, and I had no way of expressing it to anyone but myself) would be an understatement, especially since Mateo—the band's promoter— only played bass during one song. But despite how awkward or random the experience was, it is embossed in my memory.

Cádiz

Miguel Ángel quickly became my surrogate father in Spain. His daughter was studying abroad in Poland for the year, so he filled this void with guaranteeing my well-being instead. Whenever I took a trip, Alberto and he would both warn me to be careful, echoing the universal fear of a parent for a child traveling alone through the unknown realms of the "dangerous" world. But these advisements fell on deaf ears.

Fear was useless against my shield of invincibility.

In order to do what I intended to do—travel alone through foreign territories—I had to trust that everything would be okay no matter where I went or who I met.

Naturally, the exploration of Spain was first on my travel agenda, but boasting a cornucopia of desirable destinations, I had no sense of where to begin.

One of my former teaching assistants, Blake, had written a letter of recommendation for me as part of the application process with TEACH. A request that revealed the fabric of a deeper connection.

He had lived in Spain himself for almost ten years.

I contacted him, requesting his expert input.

Hola guapa!

*How are you liking it? Since you are in the South, you
must travel to Cádiz to meet my best friend, Víctor. I am
certain he would love nothing but to show you around. I will
email the both of you together, so you can make the proper
arrangements.*

Ciao!

Blake

Víctor emailed me personally, inviting me to stay with him for a
few days.

While Shayna went to Granada with friends from TEACH, I
embarked on a preliminary couchsurfing adventure with someone
who wasn't a full-blown stranger in a town I knew nothing about.

I got into Cádiz by train at around eleven o'clock in the evening,
inconveniencing my gracious host with the task of picking me up.
But he would hear nothing of my apologies.

"Don't do that," he said in English.

I asked, "Could we please speak in Spanish a bit? I really want to
pract—"

"Well, that depends. Are you any good?"

He smirked to ensure that I understood his sarcasm.

When we got to his apartment, we snacked on shortbread cookies
beneath the harsh lighting at the bistro table in his kitchen. He
explained that he coached an orienteering team that had practice
the following morning.

He specified the term in response to my blank expression. "It's
capture the flag but in the forest. Would you rather sleep in or come
along?"

I say 'yes' to everything.

"I'd love to go."

"Okay. See you at six-thirty."

We ate a quick breakfast of toast with olive oil and Nespresso coffee before heading out to pick up a student from the school where Víctor taught.

The student, Ingrid, happened to be female, and, although I trusted Víctor, it was difficult for me not to question the parental involvement in the matter. I'm sure her parents did not know I would be coming, meaning my presence did not influence whether or not their high school–aged daughter could drive alone with a male teacher.

I had experienced enough blurring of lines between discipline and intimate care at Colegio de San José—little girls running with their shirts pulled over their heads warranted an affirmative reaction from the teachers, "¡Qué linda!"—that I ultimately deduced Spanish culture as less politically correct and more familial than American.

The cement in a corner of my heart cracked.

The judgments I held were not mine but were byproducts of a scattered culture I had spent twenty-two years absorbing. A culture predicated on fearing others: i.e. Native Americans, Mexicans, African Americans, or men if you are a woman. Trust between relative strangers was not dead. That was just another American myth disguised as reality.

We drove the thirty minutes to Cañas de Meca, an iconic surf spot, famous for its seemingly endless golden sand.

The beach faded into a glimmer in the distance as we climbed the mountainside into the expansive forest of La Breña Natural Park. We pulled into the parking lot, where the rest of the participants stood awaiting our arrival. Víctor hurried to pair us up so we could begin, handing each couple a map and a compass. He paired me with Ingrid, who also happened to be a beginner at this sport.

The competition was timed, and the goal was to reach each of the eleven checkpoints sprinkled throughout the forest and return to the beginning before the other teams.

Go!

I had been so caught up in Víctor's haste to start the match that I didn't even think to voice that I didn't know how to read a map or use a compass, the only skills necessary to participate.

Ingrid and I attempted to collaborate, looking at the map, comparing trees we saw in relation to the starting point on the map. Certain borders were depicted with hash marks, but the only other written symbols were checkpoint numbers.

After a while of searching for the first checkpoint, we decided that we would both prefer to just enjoy the scenery rather than figure out how to decipher the cryptic guide.

We began to wander aimlessly, passing by a tour of three people on horseback, walking by the horses as closely as one would another human. I realized that I hadn't noticed a designation of paths that separated the humans from the horses from the dogs. Nor were there any signs specifying *Pick up after your dog* or *Dog must be on a leash.* This was unadulterated nature through which both man and beast were free to traverse and carve their own paths.

Lost in splendor, we hiked to a breach where it was high enough to take in the panoramic view of Mother Nature's infinite terrestrial sculpture. The glassy blue sparkled as if the ocean was heaven's earthly reflection. The majesty of our surroundings left us silent at times, hypnotized without regard for time, distance, or the essentials for survival. The purity of nature's womb had transfixed our souls.

We roamed further, hopping a fence, eventually approaching a micro-neighborhood of three houses where a few cows grazed, thrusting us out of our mutual daydream.

Ingrid shook her head. "This looks wrong."

I had just been thinking about how grateful I was to be paired with Ingrid, who had been willing to talk to me in Spanish (because she didn't know English). But now that instinct mode was kicking in, the art of conversation dissipated. Urgency converted time back into the inescapable construct by which we conduct life.

The first dose of relief came when we found the fence we had hopped, but it wasn't until we walked along the fence for what seemed like miles that we arrived at an opening.

We decided to turn right, but the trail quickly narrowed and lost its markings. We both agreed that we had gone the wrong way, picking up our pace in the opposite direction.

The threat of survival was a rapid devolution from domestic to wild.

Without thinking, our beings had shifted into that of wolves.

Our minds functioned on identifying the subtle irregularities amid the homogeneous territory. Moving swiftly but cautiously. Hopeless exhaustion was on the verge of setting in when we both spotted a break in the distance. We paused to confer with each other, trading a smile. Connected by our mutual will to stay alive, language had become obsolete in this intuitive nerve network that alerted us both to break into a sprint toward the wall of light against the trees.

We turned to smile at one another again, releasing celebratory yelps, pushing our bodies as fast as we could toward the safety of the familiar. We broke through the barrier of brush onto the shoulder of a highway. We were in between the breeze of cars speeding by and the spirit of the wolf that was unable to cross from one world to the next. The approaching sound of a car scared our internal guides away. A couple from Víctor's orienteering group pulled up, assuring us that we were close.

"*Gracias!* How long have we been gone?" asked Ingrid.

"Six hours."

"*Lo siento,*" I apologized.

"*No te preocupes.* We are just glad you are both safe."

We made the quickest leg of our journey back, jogging along the shoulder of the road until we turned the corner into the parking lot. Víctor glanced over. His empty expression was instantly filled with joyous relief. He rushed over, squeezing me into his chest, profusely lamenting for having put me in danger.

He was shaking out his fear with every word, but I couldn't help but laugh.

"Víctor. Do not worry at all! That was the most accidental fun I have ever had."

Granada

The following weekend, we had another national holiday at school, affording me four days to realize my first official Couchsurfing.com experience in the historic city of Granada.

I would travel four hours by bus to meet my host, Marco, late on Friday evening after he finished a wine tasting with his parents.

He was boyishly cute (derived by his profile picture), Spanish, and had traded introductory Whatsapps with me—concerning our mutual affinity for music—a week before I had arrived.

We formally met around eight-thirty p.m. at a bar, exchanging the customary kisses on each cheek. He was shorter than I with an ethnically ambiguous face—light blue eyes offset his dark hair—and a beard, accenting his hipster fashion.

"How was your trip?"

No, this sentence has not been translated from Spanish to English. His accent even sounded American.

I actively swallowed my disappointment.

Why had Víctor and, now, Marco both insisted on speaking to me in English?

I am here to learn Spanish and be uncomfortable in my
ability to communicate.

While walking to his apartment to drop off my things, I had to ask.
"Is there any way we could speak Spanish?"

He rambled off something indecipherable as if he was
intentionally saying a phrase I would not be able to understand.

"Uh. *Pero, despacio, por favor.*"

He chuckled to himself.

"We will see how the night goes. I just think it's weird for me to
speak to you in Spanish because I work with tons of foreigners and
we all speak English to one another. Not Spanish."

I considered this.

"You will meet them tomorrow."

We stopped in front of a large door down a darkened alley. I had
not paid much attention to our trajectory due to my preoccupations
with one of my prerequisites—speak Spanish—for this trip.

His cozy one-bedroom apartment was uncharacteristically clean
for a bachelor. He stood in the doorframe while I put my things by
the couch. I paused in brief consideration over whether I should
bring my phone or not. Due to the hour, we needed to go because
the bars were approaching maximum capacity, and impulsively
craving the liberation that comes with being disconnected from
technology, I left my phone.

After *tapas* and beer, we were walking down the street when
Marco spotted someone he knew. A jolly, round German fellow
trailing a pack of friends, all of whom were much further along in
their alcoholic consumption than us.

He and Marco were gregariously talking when Marco followed
him into the bar behind them. Waving me along felt like an
afterthought. The doorway of the establishment framed his compact
stature, leaving me no choice but to grudgingly follow.

Marco seemed to be more of a "group guy" than a "one-on-

*one guy," quickly trading time with me for this unforeseen
circumstance.*

The German ordered a round of *chupitos,* and I became a
wallflower to the boisterous festivities unfolding around me. We
took shots, everyone much more enthusiastically than I, before
mobilizing back into the brisk fall air.

Marco was a few paces in front of me, commandeering the way,
when he recognized someone else in the street. A tall, skinny guy
dressed in simple street clothes with deeply darkened skin one
could get lost in. Marco excitedly embraced him as I approached his
side, subtly demanding a formal introduction this time.

"This is Khalish."

We did the customary kiss on the cheek exchange before Marco
and Khalish resumed their accidental reunion, fervently walking
and talking, advancing paces ahead of the rest of the group.

I resolved that he probably wanted alone time with what seemed
to be a close friend, so I began talking to one of the girls in the
German group who could still formulate coherent sentences. But,
by the next time I glanced ahead, Khalish and Marco had rounded a
corner and vanished out of sight.

"Hold on."

I abandoned Gerta, mid-sentence, running to the corner they
had turned down, mindful not to lose the German girls as well. I
approached an empty street, absent of any sign of them.

The daze of alcohol was expunged.

My heart was desperately grasping at sparse wisps of reassurance
so as not to fall into the pit of my nervous stomach.

I ran back to Gerta.

"They're gone. My friends are gone."

Gerta and crew were unfazed.

"Why don't you just call them?"

"I didn't bring my phone."

"Do you know where he lives?"

"No, I just got here maybe three hours ago."

"Well, that was dumb of you."

Unable to swallow the helplessness of my situation, I began to sob. The possibility of something going wrong during one of my solo adventures was presently occurring.

How could I have put such blind faith in a stranger to look out for me?

I should have been paying more attention, asking more questions, and looking out for myself. Self-loathing looped through my head. Once Gerta saw that I was crying, she reluctantly offered to let me stay with her. I was imagining myself at this new destination, still without any way of locating Marco ever again when my reel of negativity was interrupted.

"Hey!"

I turned around to Marco swiftly trekking up the hill to the church we had stopped by.

"Are you crying?"

He was talking to me like a calloused father.

"No..."

I turned my face away to hide my tears when he grabbed my cheeks, jerking my face toward him.

"You *were* crying. Well, why did you lose us then?"

"I was talking. I didn't realize you two were going to run away!"

"Yeah, yeah. Keep up then."

We parted ways from a night of untapped potential thanks to my getting lost (again).

Walking back in silence, my mind obsessively unraveled.

I couldn't tell if Marco liked me or if he was thinking that he had made a huge mistake by allowing me to stay with him.

I reviewed the evolution of the night, gathering data, comparing variables, when I found our source of incompatibility.

I had expected him to be catering to my every whim rather than going along with whatever was presented.

I was more self-conscious than usual.

This constant shuffle between new places, sometimes occurring in multiple foreign languages, was enough to set my guard up; but, also, removing the buffer of a hostel or hotel—where accommodations are standardized, serving as a momentary refuge from culture shock—is downright exposing.

But that's why Couchsurfing.com had intrigued me in the first place.

I wanted to immerse myself in each cultural setting via the most realistic place of all.

A person's life.

No, it was not ideal, but I was not searching for the ideal. I was searching for the raw, real, uncut version of what it means to be alive.

The next morning, we awoke to rainfall, cleansing my palette of the night before. We drank the standard Nespresso at home before heading out down the alley. Marco toted an umbrella, and I deliberately carried both my phone and childlike wonder.

"So, we're going to a hotel for a food tasting."

"Uh..."

"One of my friend's boyfriends is opening a new restaurant and is being featured along with a few other chefs."

The universe strikes again. I let go, and it responds with the unimaginable and the unexpected.

Footsteps muddled the grime against the hollow city streets. Marco was quiet. I understood that now. My thoughts became an ambient soundtrack of objectivity, such as the urban parallels between Granada and Seville differing from the hippie beach town of Cádiz.

The swanky hotel abruptly commanded my attention as Marco confidently climbed the stairs toward the lobby.

It was also no longer surprising that Marco recognized the first people we saw in the coat check line. Curtis and Olivia.

Curtis was American, and Olivia, his petite, blonde-haired girlfriend, was Swedish. They were both coworkers of Marco's—welcoming and sweet—who had been invited to the tasting as well.

We eventually forged forces with the rest of the crew: the Polish Rufin and the chef's girlfriend, Lucia. Each of us clutched our eleven a.m. beers, exchanging small talk between samples of modern renditions of traditional Spanish *tapas*.

After the soiree, Marco invited everyone over to his parents' house for coffee and gin and tonics (a Spanish cocktail favorite) since his parents had left town for the weekend. The party grew with the late addition of Khalish and a French student on Erasmus, Ali, shortly after we had settled into this new locale.

We were two Americans, two Spaniards, a Pole, a Frenchman, and a Moroccan ex-pat; a smörgåsbord if I had ever seen one. Our level of familiarity—established earlier at the hotel—and comfort level—enhanced by the effects of alcohol—bred an expansive array of topics discussed, from politics to philosophy to music. Everyone—with the exception of Marco and Lucia—was speaking in their second or third language—Spanish—as I sunk into the cushion of the couch. A smile effortlessly spread across my face

I had arrived.

We groggily arose around lunch time the next morning with plans to meet Curtis and Olivia at a restaurant across from the Alhambra, the historic Moorish-erected gem of Granada.

Sunlight penetrated the previous day's depleted clouds, enlivening the history around us, inspiring Marco to penetrate through the silence I had grown so accustomed to as well.

"So, you know Khalish, right? Well, he grew up in Morocco and started working at an early age. He was a cab driver by the time he was fifteen. One day, a man got into his cab, engaging Khalish in conversation. He asked him questions about his family, his age, and things like this. Questions that were not customary for a passenger to inquire about. Khalish told him that he worked to help take care of his family and, because of this, would not be able to continue school for much longer. At the end of the ride, the man gave Khalish his phone number and said, 'If you are ever in Granada, call me, and you will have a job.' Two years later, that's exactly what he did... Yep. *And* the guy from the cab remembered Khalish. He gave him a place to sleep in his house, but, in order to work for the man, Khalish had to enroll in university. *I know.* So he works at the man's mansion part-time and is a student for the remainder."

It was one of those fundamental stories that a person like Khalish would never share about himself. When interacting with him, although I had seen his goodness, I had overlooked his humility.

Marco answered his cell phone, organizing where we would meet Curtis, as I took in the landscape that set our new scene. Gray cobblestone, uneven and worn, cradled my feet. Antiquated stone walls bordered the streets from the deep valleys that climbed into high mountains. One's gaze naturally followed the picturesque trees offsetting the rich, sand-colored fortress of the Alhambra.

L unch naturally flowed along more meaningful channels than the topical conversation from the day before.

Curtis found comfort in my Americanism, confiding his story of being the adopted Asian child of a white family in Georgia.

"I never felt like I was different from my parents, but that didn't stop other people from thinking so."

The *duende*, the unconscious flow of allowing the universe to guide me to that which magnetized me, had led me to a man who had initially not wanted to engage with me but possessed a wealth of significant friendships I needed to engage with.

Curtis and Khalish, with objectively far more difficult situations than I, were not complaining about where they came from. Life was not arduous to them. Challenge wasn't even recognizable. It was just a part of it.

Somehow, after attending an impromptu jazz festival that morphed into smoking hash outside the Alhambra, I ended up sleeping in the same bed as Marco that night.

Nothing happened beyond a welcomed cuddling, but when he dropped me off the next morning at the bus station, he acted as if it had never happened.

I Whatsapped my friend from home, confused by what it all had meant.

Would he text me? Would he want to see me again?

I needed validation. I needed comprehension. The dynamics of the female-male world were a mystery to me.

Was I able to fall in love with everyone I met? If so, why didn't other people want to do the same?

When it came to men, I did not understand the proper etiquette. I did not understand the intricacy of a random hook up. I did not understand how to play the game.

Integration

While making preparations for my 14-day trip through Paris, Amsterdam, Berlin, and Bruges over Christmas break, Shayna casually swayed into the living room with tomato juice trickling down her chin (incurred from biting into a beefsteak tomato like an apple), draping herself atop the chair next to mine.

"So, where ya goin' on your trip?"

"Um…"

I gave her the quick rundown without any additional detail.

"You know, I was thinking…"

Oh fucking no.

"I have a few extra nights before Jenny meets me in Santander. I was actually planning on going to Paris alone, too. But it makes way more sense if we go together."

It was November, and I assumed that it was obvious that our initial union had been one of convenience.

I traveled alone to see what happened along the way, while she stayed in hostels with the same American friends she had met through TEACH.

To be with other Americans, labeled as tourists, infiltrating borrowed streets, deliberately making our existence known, made me cringe. I was still on the pursuit of blending in with the foreign landscape, extracting myself from compromising with other people's needs, all the while establishing my own route. But despite my extreme methods, I wasn't immune to flashes of longing for home. There were spontaneous mental exhalations of frustration whenever I craved the luxury of my car, independently maneuvering from place to place, safely detached from others within a metal barrier of music and wandering thoughts. The previously unappreciated ease of my American life stemmed from the fact that I walked everywhere. The train station was a forty-five-minute walk away, during which I contemplated the ubiquity of compact cars, highways without traffic, and no one drinking coffee or eating a muffin on the go. The scale and style of modern America could never fit here. But I was in Spain, not America. I was not here to compare, I was here to adapt.

So I took Shayna's proposal into greater consideration.

We would stay together in Paris.

Thanksgiving was four days away, and my ache for familiarity was at an unprecedented high. While on Facebook during my lunch break, I came across a picture of my friend Carrie from high school posing by the Guadalquivir River in Seville.

I took this happenstance as a sign.

> **Me:** *OMG! You're here! I only live an hour away. Let's do something!*

She quickly messaged me back, and we organized a rendezvous for the following day.

I could only stay for the afternoon because Alma and her sister, Magdalena, were helping me prepare Thanksgiving at their house the next morning. But I wouldn't need much longer than that anyway. It was the first time I would be returning to Seville since my homestay.

I met Carrie and Carrie's friend, Britt, in the Triana neighborhood for drinks and *tapas*.

I was trying to swallow my enthusiasm for this coveted interaction with someone from home. Someone who not only had a frame of reference for who I used to be but someone relatively normal who could benefit from the entertainment provided by the last three months of my life.

Hours of stories felt like minutes when Carrie graciously cut me off after looking at her phone.

"Cee. I'm so sorry, but we actually have to get back to the hotel to meet up with my mom."

"Of course. Yes."

We settled up the tab and walked back across the bridge before parting ways.

"Thank you so much for letting me come see you."

I gave Carrie the warmest hug I could, stifling the urge to not let go.

"Wait. You should just come with us."

My heart elevated.

"No. It's okay. You should spend time with your mom."

"She doesn't care. She's here with her boyfriend. Just come back and have a drink with us."

"Are you sure?"

"Yes! Come."

Her mom was more than welcoming and even invited me to tag along further for dinner. An offer to prolong this fragrance of familiarity that was too tempting to refuse.

After a lavish dinner, my profuse gratitude was not enough to convey my appreciation.

I had to offer them something they couldn't find anywhere else.

The nightlife of Spain.

I whisked the girls toward Calle Alfalfa, hoping to run into the Spanish tour guides from TEACH. And, just as I'd intended, Rafael and Marco were loitering outside with two friends unaffiliated with the program. Oscar and (new) Rafael.

A glaringly positive aspect of Marco and Rafael was their respect for American women, always erring on the side of platonic silliness. But the same could not be said for new Rafael. Due to their mutual fluency in English, Rafael and Marco were entertaining Carrie and Britt while (new) Rafael tested my Spanish aptitude.

Even though I knew he was from Seville, I admitted that it was not my favorite city. A sentiment that was always means for gasps and admonishments.

"How could you not like Seville? We are the best city in all of Andalucía! No, no—in all of Spain!"

For the second time that day, I recalled my homestay, explaining to him the family dynamics and where they lived.

"They weren't Spanish, *hombre!* That's why! They were foreigners living here. Also, that is the worst neighborhood of Seville. There is no action there."

I took notice of how much he cared. He not only listened but dissected the story.

After chatting inside over a round of drinks, I popped out to check on Carrie and Britt.

"Hey, you guys okay?"

They were both bright red, grinning all too big, their eyelids casting shadows below their irises.

"I think we're gonna head back."

Their legs haphazardly caught their top-heavy torsos mid–involuntary sway.

"Do you want me to walk with you?"

"No, no. It's okay. Come back to the room whenever you want. Room 203."

They floated into the vacant night as I briefly noted Carrie's accidental, but impactful, inclusion in my Spanish life.

Rafael laughed from behind my shoulder in their wake.

"Where are they going? It's still early!"

I was not sure what time the girls left, but Rafael and I were the last ones to leave Calle Alfalfa.

He walked me back to the hotel through the empty streets of Seville. Plazas that I had only seen occupied were made private by moonlight when, the next thing I knew, Rafael and I were vigorously making out on top of a parked car. His hand crawled beneath my shirt, advancing our relationship at lightning speed. The program had warned us to be prudent with Spanish men, for they were known to pick up visiting American girls and dispose of them as soon as they finished. But from what I had gathered, Rafael was a good guy. It was the *chupitos* of tequila that had gotten the best of us.

I pushed his hand out and he pulled away.

"You want to stop?"

"Yeah. I really need to get back. What time is it?"

"Six."

Oh my god.

I had a train to catch in four hours. I had to be sober enough to translate Thanksgiving recipes into Spanish and then physically prepare them.

Rafael walked me to the entrance of the hotel without any more detours.

"I will call you."

After Marco from Granada never spoke to me again, my new approach to men would be apathy.

I had also been drunk, meaning no true attachments had formed.

Plus, I still was recovering from my Sevillan homestay family trauma.

I wasn't even sure if I liked it here.

I tiptoed into the hotel room to the harmony of two snoring girls passed out atop the covers of the sole king size bed. I arranged throw pillows along the floor into a makeshift cot, snagging the last

unused towel from the bathroom to use as a blanket. I set my alarm
for eight-thirty to ensure a coffee before my walk to the train.

I woke up to four text messages from Rafael, immediately
Whatsapping my friend from home to relay the unintentional
success with this guy from Seville.
 "Until six in the morning! Are you crazy?"
 I smirked at this.
 I did feel a little crazy.

Alma and Magdalena picked me up from the train station on
their way to the grocery store.
 There were only two markets in town, both of which did not
sell whole turkeys, so I had to think on my feet. We resolved to
preparing individual turkey breasts stuffed with chestnuts and
cranberries along with the planned mashed sweet potatoes, sautéed
asparagus, stuffing, and cornbread.
 I had never made Thanksgiving dinner before, so it seemed
appropriate that it wasn't a traditional turkey and that I was on a
different continent, converting tablespoons and cups to grams and
liters, hungover, running on two hours of sleep.

Dinner was served at nine-thirty p.m.
 The novelty of Thanksgiving for my hosts had worn off
until everyone was officially summoned to the dining room.
Dumbfounded, they finally understood why it had taken so
long. The amount (and size) of dishes coupled with a delectable
presentation were two extra layers that the Spanish do not
customarily practice.
 As we passed the platters, I told them that my family normally
goes around the table to say what they are thankful for. They
processed this idea, more concerned with the food than with
interpreting the meaning, as the surmounting wave of holiday

symbolism hit me. I raised my glass, weeping through my words as I heard them aloud.

"Although I do miss my family, I am so grateful that I can call you a second family while I am here. It is very important to have a place you call home, and I finally feel like I have that with all of you."

They raised their glasses once they realized my level of emotion, thanking me for the meal, when it was I who was indebted to them.

They had provided both the space (I managed to only break Alma's microwave door handle and one of the knobs on her oven) and the resources necessary to replicate a makeshift version of my own tradition. A tradition that was loaded with mixed emotions.

Despite the coveted distance between my family and me, the weight of their presence was still with me. Ironically, the only person I had shared anything personal with in town had been Alberto. Mostly because one of our lessons fell on the heels of a conversation with my mother. A conversation concerning a potentially cancerous cyst in her breast. Prompting an agonizing week of pre-result prayer mania during which my potential reality reverted back to my greatest fear.

*Not only would my time realizing my dream be cut short,
but it would be cut short to repeat the past. To take care of a
person who cannot take care of herself.*

It was complicated.

It was complicated that they missed me while my mind told me I didn't feel the same way as my heart argued otherwise. For as much as I didn't miss their penetration of my emotional well-being, there was a dependence there as inherent as the need to breathe.

Her results were benign, but its positive outcome did not eclipse the reminder from where I came. If anything, it emphasized the impossibility of escaping my bloodline. The lifelong umbilical cord between her and me was not an earthly choice; therefore, I could not interpret what it meant at that time. All I could do was take the threat of my departure into my depths, using it to stoke the flames of my appreciation.

After three hours of second and third helpings, Alberto retrieved the Pedro Ximénez from the wine cellar. I was not sure that my body could absorb any more alcohol, but it was homemade, and the refusal of homemade dessert wine in any Latin man's home is practically illegal.

"When are we going on a bike ride, Alberto?"

Alberto was always talking about his bike rides when recapping our weekends to one another during lessons. I had been pestering him to invite me for a few months now, having hinted that bike rides were a favorite pastime of my father's and mine multiple times.

"Do you want to go tomorrow?"

"Uh…"

"We will leave at seven in the morning."

I normally would not entertain the idea of another night with less than six hours of sleep, but…

"Okay."

"Okay, six-thirty it is!"

"Alberto!"

He cackled. "Seven is fine."

He licked the palm of his hand and gave me a high-five, his signature move after making some sort of joke, the majority of which were lost in translation.

A mere five hours later, I woke up to my alarm, nursing the hangover of the century.

I could not bear the thought of putting anything else in my stomach and groggily shuffled over to Alberto's house.

"Are you alright?"

"Thanks, Alberto."

"It's okay. If you can't make it all the way, Alma can drive and pick us up."

I had assumed this would be a light cruise through Peñaflor but brought my phone and ear buds just in case. An intuitive move. Alberto had packed his mp3 player as well.

We mounted our respective mountain bikes, leaving the sleeping town in our wake as I trailed Alberto's lead. He took us through the town using side streets, crossing the bridge out of Peñaflor onto a two-lane street surrounded by nothing but brush on either side. Alberto pointed to the large mountain in the distance. We were riding to the nearby nature park, Los Cabezos, for my first point of contact with the immediate surroundings of Peñaflor.

Alberto peeked over his shoulder. He maintained a strong stride, about one bike size ahead of me.

"You good?"

"Yeah," I cheerfully lied.

The distance was deceiving. It took thirty minutes for us to arrive at the beginning of the trail.

Alberto did not even bother acting like he would try to keep pace with me as we began the alternation between climb and descent along a dusty road, used by both vehicle and bike, through the mountain.

Before living here, I would have never assumed that Spain possessed as many of the primitive, natural settings that I had been exposed to. A handful of signs notifying what type of game was permissible to hunt passed by as we swiftly glided through cork oaks and wove around in an immeasurable inward spiral. The numbness in my legs had been offset by the fluid stream of ionizing air. After two hours, Alberto finally slowed to a stop at the edge of a heather-purple lake protected by a circular fortress of rocky peaks.

Alberto stared into the mountains' reflection rippling across the face of the water. No one else had been on the trail or was present at this ethereal resting point. His arsenal of jokes had been left at home alongside the stress of work demands and adult responsibility. He had finally relented and brought me here. A place he had never spoken of and would never speak of again.

The place where he found peace.

The following week came, and I did not hear from Rafael.
I went to my regularly scheduled class with Alberto, profusely expressing my thanks for the bike ride from the week prior. He just smiled without carrying the sentiment further. But there was more immediate novelty abreast capturing my attention.

A new family for *clases particulares.*

The mother was a surgeon, and the father owned and managed the only organic orange and grapefruit groves in town. Yet, somehow, they were extremely active in their three recreationally involved children's lives: Nuria, Carlos, and Jordi. Nuria was the eldest daughter, pale and blonde, athletic and studious. Carlos was the awkward middle child who intermittently distracted himself by looking out the window or doodling on his page, a practice of resistance to any extracurricular lesson that wasn't *futbol.* Jordi, the youngest, was not my student yet always sat in the background of my lessons with his siblings. Most days, he left the house during the middle of our lesson, waving goodbye with a guitar case strapped to his back, the neck hovering six inches above his head.

The majority of the families I tutored had mothers with jobs that allowed them to be home after school and kids who neither participated in extracurricular activities nor held interest in their studies.

Thus, their progressive approach to Spanish life was noteworthy.

After only two lessons, I couldn't help but shower Antonia, the mother, with compliments.

It was a rare moment to see her home, thus I felt compelled to voice the obscure connection I felt to her family.

"Antonia? I would love to get to know you and your family better if you ever have time on the weekend to have lunch together."

I had nothing to lose.

"Okay. We have games on Saturday, but on Sunday we are having lunch in the *campo*."

"Oh. Okay."

I assumed that that was her way of diverting the answer. But, in reaction to my stupor, she specified, "So, do you want to come?"

Ah—the language barrier!

I occasionally misinterpreted implications.

"Yes! I would love that!"

"Okay. I will text you on Sunday."

I felt a tiny victory. I was expanding my Spanish web, bouncing toward my next lesson when Rafael texted me.

Rafael: *Do you want to visit me this weekend? :)*

Even though I had just made plans with Antonia, I did not want to decline Rafael.

Me: *Where would we stay?*

Rafael still lived with his parents, like many post-graduate Spaniards do.

Rafael: *I'll pick you up from the train station. We have a house in Mataslacañas, a beach town a few hours outside Seville."*

Oh, how I missed the beach!

Oh, how I could not refuse a one-night beach rendezvous with a Spanish man who wanted to whisk me away!

Me: *I would love to.*

Rafael picked me up from the train station in his compact European car.

"So, how are the *campesinos sin dientes*?"

He often poked fun at where I lived, having not known Peñaflor existed until we met.

I was putting on my seatbelt as he handed me a CD case of homemade burnt discs, the majority of which were adorned with **DJ RAYMAN**, to choose from.

"That's me."

I smirked, not necessarily knowing what to expect on any of these CDs.

"I went through a big electronic phase," he said, which was exactly what was on the CD I had chosen at random. However, it faded into the background as I spoke to him in Spanish, frequently pausing due to his interruptions, correcting every other sentence I uttered. Finally, I shot him an annoyed glare.

"What? You want to speak properly, don't you?"

We stopped at the local market to buy pork chops for dinner before arriving at his parents' bungalow.

Sand enlivened the vacant concrete walkway. Bars situated along the same real estate as sunbathers were closed for the winter, setting an uncharacteristic tone for any beach town I'd ever frequented in SoCal.

Forgotten.

"Very few people live here full-time, and most people won't be back until summer," Rafael said after I commented on the sparse patronage at the market.

My spirit calmed from slow saline inhalations while Rafael handled all the items necessary for our enjoyment—opening the windows, assembling the charcoal barbecue, and uncorking a bottle of wine—without ever looking to me for help.

He taught me the Spanish trick for delicious pork chops— rosemary plucked from the garden—and how to prepare potatoes like his mother had taught him. We sat at the dining table, candles lit, as we drank red wine, and I asked him about being a lawyer in Spain. We cuddled on the couch in our pajamas, watching a dubbed version of *The Matrix Reloaded*. And, the following morning, a warm smiling body made me coffee before taking my hand to shuffle along the unobstructed shoreline.

Our walk along the sibylline ocean acted as a concealed language portal. Normally, I had to stand on my tippy toes, extending my fingertips to find the vocabulary necessary for translating feelings into words. But that day was uncharacteristic on all fronts. My Spanish seamlessly described who I was via personal stories from home, and Rafael did not stop me once. He simply listened.

Although he was nine years older than me, there wasn't a palpable emphasis between his job and mine or the marriage status of his friends over mine. I was not possessed by a controlling need to put pressure on our time together or press him for details regarding his feelings about us.

There was an unspoken understanding of what our situation meant.

We were just friends.

Friends with benefits.

Antonia's husband, Carlos, picked me up from the train station the next day with little Carlos and Jordi in tow.

We were heading to the other side of Peñaflor, characterized by the rolling hills of green orange groves and open plains. We turned onto a gravel path from the two-lane highway toward a remote residence. An older gentleman was sitting on a large wooden barrel drinking a beer as we pulled into the driveway. Jordi hopped out of the car and ran toward the man. He threw his arms around the man's neck, almost knocking him over with the force of love, before bounding off again to kick a stranded soccer ball at the net in the distance. The grounds were spacious, boasting a pool, a grass area for *futbol*, and a covered patio with a long wooden table.

"Cee!"

Antonia emerged from their classic Spanish home with creamy stucco walls and a clay tile roof, beaming as she ran up to greet me.

"Come! Let me show you."

Both Carlos's parents—the man at the gate was his father—and

Antonia's parents were there, along with her cousin, his wife, and their two children, Isabella and David. I didn't get much of a chance to engage with anyone because Antonia led me away on a tour.

They had only been able to preserve the wood-beam ceilings as part of the original infrastructure of their colonial weekend home on a lot ripe with Roman ruin relics. Two sixteen-foot clay vases stood as bookends on either side of the entry gate to their premises. They had once been in the ground, naturally preserving olive oil and wine at cooler temperatures.

"Do you want to go pick oranges?"

We headed across the street to a terrestrial sea of verdant orange trees.

I had only picked oranges once before with Patricia and Rodrigo when Shayna and I first arrived in Peñaflor. Antonia and Carlos were just as giving, encouraging me to take as many oranges home with me that I picked. The children casually trampled through the configuration of trees amidst my engrossment with the depth of every leaf and the invigorating scent of every plump orange, picking significantly less fruit than possible.

It was moments such as these that were impossible to process, much less convey.

This was the family Eduardo had mentioned when I first arrived to Colegio de San José; but, for some reason, they had taken almost two months to contact me. By the time we met, I felt more secure, both professionally with my private lessons and personally, in speaking as bluntly as I had with Antonia, which had gotten me to this current point.

The divine formation of multiple forces colliding to make this level of perfection possible were indescribable, as was the amount of Spanish happening around me.

I had only been in small groups of people who understood my situation and deliberately enunciated when in my presence. Without a similar cognizance, the elders' Spanish was practically garbled when telling the stories of the past over lunch at the regal setting outside. Their comments required a shared context I could not draw upon; so I blended in with the atmosphere to witness familial synergy in its most authentic form.

Immediately following our meal, we removed our chairs from the table to face the opposite direction, where David, Antonia's middle-aged cousin, sat with his guitar. He faced the fading sun, his messenger hat shading only his forehead, as he cradled his instrument, closed his eyes, and began to sing.

After a few Spanish folk songs, he placed the guitar in Jordi's lap. Jordi sheepishly blushed and shook his head, but it was of no use. After a few roars of insistence, he propped the guitar on his knee and assumed the somber tone of flamenco. His proficiency made me question his age.

> *A nine year old with such discipline and talented, quick plucking from memory?*

Who were these freaks of Spanish nature?

It grew cold as the sun disappeared, so we moved inside for coffee and dessert. Family members who had missed lunch began filtering through the newly shut doors, seemingly unannounced but warmly received nonetheless. I felt even more out of place as the family festivities grew in both number and sound. I spotted Isabella safely removed against the wall by the kitchen and meandered over.

"What's up?"

She politely grinned and shrugged.

"What do you do here?"

"I just graduated from school in Seville, so I just moved back home."

I cut her off, unable to restrain my enthusiasm.

"What a coincidence! I just graduated, too!"

She nodded and smiled politely.

"Well, we should hang out then."

"Yeah. Maybe."

"Do you have WhatsApp?"

"Everyone has WhatsApp," she laughed.

"So what's your number?"

She reluctantly texted me her number, but after just one afternoon for coffee, we were frequently seen together in town.

I became busier than ever with the expansion of my social realm sparked by these new relationships with Rafael and Isabella.

Once every couple weeks, I would go to Seville to visit Rafael, indulging in the liveliness of city nights that extended into the early morning. A juxtaposition to my alternate weekends spent with Isabella's family and friends barbecuing at Los Cabezos on Saturdays and extended lunches at her grandmother's house on Sundays.

It was happening.

I was becoming Spanish.

The only person I could shamelessly share these success stories with was the only person who could objectively measure my growth against the original me from two months ago.

Alberto.

"We need to go back to Los Cabezos on a bike ride again," I told him.

I did not want my first established relationship, that with Alberto and his generous family, to slip into the ether.

"We can't do that anymore, Cee."

His expression was void.

He had been uncharacteristically sullen for a couple of weeks now. Ever since his father had fallen ill, he was managing three businesses at once. But I could not tap into his submersion of stress.

"Why not?"

He sighed.

Surely, his English lessons were a superfluous task that could have shifted to the back-burner, yet he never canceled.

"Because I am very public in this town. Everyone knows who I am, and people talk."

"Oh."

The pieces of the puzzle were sliding into place.

A couple weeks back, Alberto had requested that we meet at his office for our English lessons instead of his house. I had initially assumed that he had changed the location because it was easier for him to stay at work.

"Alma doesn't think it's a good idea," I finally confirmed.

I could not resist being clear because this stipulation did not sound like it was coming from him.

"We can meet for lessons."

For at least a month now, I could feel the old pieces of myself—the old resentments about the way I looked and people's judgments of me based upon my appearance—whirling down the drain into the abyss. So it shouldn't have come as a surprise; this timely blockage sending the frustrations flooding back in. But I did not look at Alma's disapproval as a test from the universe—its way of seeing if I indeed had let those pieces of myself go—because I was still too triggered by the piece itself. Even though this woman knew me, having spent time alone with me, something about me made her feel uncomfortable with her husband and I spending time together.

I saw how it could be perceived by others, but it was unfair.

Alberto's and my friendship was threatened by appearances as opposed to concrete reasoning. Clearly, no one could understand the closeness that I had developed with this person, not by age or gender but by us both being honest versions of ourselves.

I didn't push the issue further but felt the same pain of a broken friendship from back home. Compounded by factors that I could have neither predicted nor evaded.

Madrid

T he last trip I took prior to my two-week winter escapade was to Madrid.

I had contacted many people on Couchsurfing.com, requesting to be hosted, but it wasn't until the day before I left that someone accepted me. He was a college student living in a house with four other students, and he taught music and played in a band. Due to his busy schedule, he wouldn't be able to act as a tour guide, but that did not hold as much importance to me anymore. The Spanish capital was an obligatory destination either way.

I began my cold winter journey on a walk to breakfast, when one of the other hosts, Martín, who had initially declined my request, messaged me. He asked me if I would like to have a picnic in the park later that afternoon, and I impulsively accepted. It wasn't until I walked a bit further that my unconscious reply sunk in. I didn't even really remember who this guy was or what he did. I was walking faster now, deciding that I could cancel if I changed my mind.

M adrid was dark, grandiose, and bustling.

There was a corporate and rushed pull unlike that of the nostalgic, pensive streets of Granada.

I had only just arrived at my first tourist attraction, the palace, when a stomachache hit. The northern cold was seeping into my bones, and, on confirmation of legitimate pain, I strongly considered abandoning this passé palace for the warmth of my bed in Peñaflor.

I WhatsApped Martín to apologize and inform him that I would be getting on the next train back home.

Martín: *You can't.*

What kind of stranger, except a sociopath, responds that way?

Me: *Yes, I can. I don't feel well, so I want to go home.*

Martín: *No. Come meet me. I will give you some paracetamol.*

Up until this point, I had taken advantage of all my potentially "ominous" offers from men and had only experienced a few logistical hiccups. None of them featured a reenactment of the movie, *Taken*, much like many people feared would occur. However, this time, I did take a longer moment to contemplate what this person was saying.

Me: *Okay. But if I don't feel better after that, you are buying me a train ticket home.*

Martín: *Yes, I will.*

I walked the twenty minutes to the address he had sent me, concentrated more on getting there and feeling better than the likelihood of this person attacking me. We met outside an apartment building. He quickly kissed each cheek before hurrying me inside. He darted up the stairwell, yelling behind him as I plodded up one step at a time.

"Come! Come!"

Once I reached the third floor, I assumed his was the apartment with the door wide open. It was a large apartment, adorned with more items than a single male could boast.

I filled in the blanks.

He lived with his parents.

"I was cooking," he yelled from the kitchen. "Come in here!"

We were speaking in English—once again—but, with my newfound friend base in the *pueblo*, I had become less neurotic about language immersion during my trips.

I entered the kitchen as he closed the door to the refrigerator.

"Okay. So what's up?"

"I don't feel well."

"Right."

Distracted, construing my comment as if it had been a command, he poured me a glass of water and retrieved the bottle of paracetamol from the pantry.

"You're going to feel better now. I've been cooking all day," he was talking in a manic fashion, too many thoughts consuming his head to relay to me all at once.

He was thinner than me, with a trimmed beard and black-rimmed glasses. He was explosive in both movement and speech, disjointedly pacing, shifting from this corner of the room to that thought before arriving at a tangential question.

"How long are you here for?"

"Today and tomorrow."

"Okay. So, we're going to a wedding."

I could not tell if he was joking or not, because he bolted out of the room again.

I took in the momentary stillness of the kitchen. Mountains of plates covered with Saran wrap were sandwiched between stocked Tupperware containers. I followed him into the living room, where he was peering outside the window.

"You're not joking."

He turned to look at me, clasping the curtain between his two fingers, dramatically emphasizing. "Why would I joke about that?"

He resumed his natural rhythm, buzzing about on the prowl for his jacket.

"They are on their way here right now. They are two artists. It is going to be at a gallery—is that all you have to wear?"

I peered down at my garb.

I was an unfittingly cold California girl with significant pain in her abdomen.

"It's fine. No one will notice." He dismissed his previous concern with a flick of his wrist as the doorbell rang.

Martín ran over to the door, revealing two men in suits who loudly embraced him amidst a clamorous exchange of Spanish. They were fashionable, I supposed, with stylish, alternative haircuts and nose rings. Martín introduced me before running into the kitchen, a form of manners I initially hadn't been sure he possessed. One of the artists picked me up while the other kissed my hand.

We grabbed as much of the food as we could carry. The Spanish between the boys was firing at the speed of bullets. Unintelligible colloquialisms whisked by me, back and forth, contributing to the natural haste with which we needed to get down to the unattended car parked illegally outside.

We all squished into the compact space of the Fiat before speeding off. Martín took a second to explain that Madrid traffic is horrible, so we would drop them off at the gallery with the food and then he and I would look for parking.

But Martín failed to give Madrid traffic its due justice. The clogged, narrow streets were impenetrable on a late Saturday afternoon. A recipe for disaster for someone like Martín who possessed a serious case of road rage. He would cut people off and insult *them* for their poor driving skills, making as many illegal turns and lane changes as possible out of the attempt to save time.

We walked twenty minutes from where we parked down a side street to the gallery, the only brilliantly lit storefront on the sleepy corridor. Elegantly dressed women and men idled outside the doors, creating a human barrier between the alley and the pristine white space.

Calling myself "underdressed" was an understatement.

Women wore fashionably small caps with veils to match their ornate, knee-length skirt suits. I kept my head down, avoiding eye contact as I moved past them inside.

Four eight-by-ten photos adorned each wall on either side of the foreground of the gallery, while the back half held the ceremony space with rows of chairs that faced toward a podium.

"Stay here. I am going to go check on the food in the back," Martín said.

"Okay…"

"Just look at the art."

He walked past the podium down a darkened hallway and disappeared behind a curtain.

I pivoted to face the first photograph on my left.

A present-day photo of both grooms lying across their mothers' laps. Both parties were nude, and the men were sucking on their respective mother's nipples. I peered around to see if anyone else viewing the art expressed any visual feedback that aligned with mine. I scooted the two steps horizontally to the next piece without successfully shaking the shock.

How had they convinced their mothers to do that?

Martín interrupted my attempt at processing the current situation.

"You think this is a gay wedding, don't you?"

I ruffled my brow, consciously lowering my voice. "What else am I supposed to think?"

"Well, it's not."

In this sole instance, I did appreciate the use of English to explain the previously misconstrued thematic content.

"How not?"

"Well, you see, they are partners. But they aren't gay. They are getting married as a part of their art installment in this gallery."

He peered over his shoulder. His friends were rehearsing in front of the podium.

"You see the blonde lady next to Cristobal? Yeah, that's his girlfriend."

The dots were connecting.

Luckily, I had started feeling better, because I could not believe that if I had gone home, I would have said no to this once in a lifetime occasion.

"They are making a commentary against the institution of marriage. If two people are in love, they should be able to get married, even best friends. Then they are going to get their marriage annulled and film their confession at the church."

"Wow."

"Yeah." He nodded knowingly. "Do you want some wine?"

"Oh my god, yes."

After the first sip of wine hit my mouth, I clumsily knocked it, spilling it onto my sweater.

"Well, if you didn't fit in before… " Martín sarcastically exclaimed.

"Okay. How do you know how to do that?"

"What?"

"Be sarcastic and funny in English."

"Oh. I used to work in hospitality in the Canary Islands. To work in hospitality, it is necessary to know English, yes? So I watched TV in English. This is probably how I know the jokes."

The ceremony was performed in Spanish, but I tuned it out, retracting into the wall, becoming just another strategic fixture placed in the exhibition.

The audience was captivated by every moment, as they would be at any ceremony. I pondered over whether anyone else thought it was odd to witness a fake gay wedding, or if it suited these two heterosexual partners, who were betrothed in the name of art. It felt accepted in a way that made it seem real, even though the Catholic Church's influence in Spain was still pervasive. I could not help but consider the difference in tone had it been an event between two lovers rather than an arrangement between two activists.

I had not showered in two days and fashioned a wine stain on my shirt, but Martín did not leave my side.

"You're pretty normal," Martín remarked.

"What's that supposed to mean?"

"I am going on a wine tour in an ancient castle tomorrow. Do you want to come?"

"Is that even a question?"

"Cool. We have to be at the bus station at seven a.m., because the bus ride takes three hours."

I trusted Martín.

"Why did you think I would be down to go to a fake wedding?"

"I didn't. I just hoped you would."

The next day, during the lengthy three-hour bus tour of northern Spain, Martín voluntarily divulged his story.

He had fallen in love with an American girl while she was visiting Málaga back when he was living there. She was a doctor and had to get back to work, but, being a romantic, he could not bear the thought of her leaving. So he booked a plane ticket and went to the hospital she worked at during one of her shifts to surprise her with his grand gesture just a mere week after she had left. She was totally freaked out and called security to escort him off the property.

I didn't know how to respond.

W e arrived at the town, which was about a tenth of the size of Peñaflor, and it began to rain. We passed by the restaurant we would be dining at later that afternoon en route to the castle.

"They serve *cordero* here. The wood oven they use to roast it is as old as the castle."

Without a clear path or any taxi service, we hiked the dampening hillside half a mile up to the castle. We checked in and were two of eight people in attendance. We both happily threw back the two glasses of wine, tried not to slide back down the hill, and muddily traipsed into the restaurant.

Warmth from the oven filled the room.

The restaurant was an antiquated farm home with both decorative and functional elements that were at least a century old.

There were only two other couples dining as a stout woman took us to our seats. The only option was a tasting menu, and so emerged a jug of wine with bread and salads, fueling Martín and me as we shifted the energy of the restaurant.

We were rowdily alternating between English and Spanish, making up hypothetical scenarios, laughing hysterically at how far we could escalate each imaginary scene. We paid and stepped foot outside the restaurant into a fiercer wind than when we had entered. We had an hour to kill in the sleepy town where everything except that restaurant was closed on Sundays. Martín put his arm through mine as we strolled around, pausing to take pictures throughout. After a few location changes, he turned and planted a kiss on my cheek, catapulting me out of our link.

The incessant stream of the weekend was finally hitting me. My craving for comfort and familiarity was peaking. And for the first time, I realized that some people you meet can be fascinating for a brief instant and that is all you need in order to leave with a satisfying taste in your mouth. But after long bouts of exposure with that same person, your whole perception of them can change.

U<small>ncharted</small> W<small>aters</small>

B<small>efore</small> embarking on my fourteen-day excursion, Isabella invited me to the annual holiday reunion she celebrated with her childhood friends.

Four other girls met us at the town's only *hambuegesería*. They were all polite and reserved, discussing mutual friends, but a notable shadow was cast on the vacant chair at the head of the table.

One of the girls groaned. "Pilar always does this."

Isabella smiled and turned to me to interpret.

"Pilar is one of those people who you have to tell to meet you two hours earlier than the actual meeting time so she will arrive at the same time as everyone else."

I smiled and nodded.

During these large get-togethers, I was so focused on not interrupting the flow of conversation that I sat in silence, simply grateful to witness intimate cultural exchanges such as these. In the off-chance that I did have a funny retort, by the time I had translated it from English to Spanish, they had already segued into another topic, one which I had entered midway, and I would have to wait until the topic switched again before understanding exactly what was going on.

About an hour later, Pilar responded to Isabella's WhatsApp, informing us that she was en route. The energy escalated with the announcement of this girl's impending arrival. After an hour of nursing watered down *ron con Coca-Colas*, the girls sat more erect, speckled with giddiness.

"Ah, Pilar!" yelled one of the girls as everyone stood up to greet her.

She was wearing a large fur coat over a mustard-yellow turtleneck sweater. I was understandably the last one in line to greet her. She approached me with a resolved confidence before kissing me on each cheek.

"Isabella's told me all about you. Do you like Peñaflor?"

"Yeah." I smiled and shrugged, not insulting her hometown while simultaneously acknowledging that it wasn't Paris.

"No, *hija*, Peñaflor's shit." She laughed, everyone else joining her, as she perched herself on her makeshift throne.

From then on, the conversation operated at peak decibels.

Pilar was the ringleader of the group. Each girl hung on her every word, having all transformed into exuberant versions of the solemn girls that I had just painstakingly endured discussing friends of friends.

After dinner, Isabella and I walked back home together.

"Just so you know, Pilar was friends with an American girl who lived here a while back, too."

I could not tell if the subtle restraint in her voice was one of warning or claim.

I just smiled. "She was nice."

Isabella recovered. "Oh, yes. She's very nice."

Shayna arrived in Paris a day earlier than I.

It had been raining, so I was wearing red rubber rain boots, which turned out to be the biggest mistake ever. The drops on the rubber were crystallizing in the cold air as I waited in a nearly empty subway station—save for a few social delinquents—at midnight. It could not have been more obvious that I was a tourist. Weary eyed, lugging an oversized roller suitcase behind me, unable to conceal the unmistakable hint that *I don't know what I am doing.*

I guess it had been a rightful initiation to watch a homeless man shoot up heroin during my ride into the city, because when I exited at my stop, I emerged into a homeless slum. Abandoned mattresses and articles of clothing strewn across the asphalt, freshly dewed, texturized the tarnished aroma that filled the air. I walked as quickly as I could to a place with streetlights, searching for the street names marked somewhere on the walls of one of the corner buildings.

Whenever I was going somewhere new, I would plot out my steps on the maps app of my iPhone—while I still had cell service or Wi-Fi—and take screenshots of the directions. I would memorize my trajectory while en route to my destination so as not to be constantly checking my phone once there and fall prey to a career pick-pocketer's well-executed plan.

After what seemed like getting lost in the labyrinth of Dante's *Inferno*—a complete neural erasure of the hearsay glamour of Paris—I hauled my suitcase up five flights of stairs to the musty greeting of our cozy Airbnb.

The next morning, Shayna's alarm went off promptly at seven. She had already planned our first day together. Before going to the Louvre, she wanted to show me the Opera House. She had gone to the ballet there during her first night here, boasting of her unforgettable experience.

We would be parting ways on the morning of the twenty-fourth, when I would be left to my own Couchsurfing.com devices. I was scheduled to stay with Clarence Waters, the only (reasonable) host available, due to the holidays. So I bought a ticket to the ballet on Christmas Eve, hedging the potential awkward Christmas Eve with a constructive excuse.

The rain fell in incessant sheets of water, an obvious deterrent from going outside for a Californian. But the distinct glow of Paris in the daylight drowned my instincts.

With every step, I gained conviction of my surroundings.

I was in the city of love, the city of Gertrude Stein, the Mecca of all artists across time. Shayna's hurried pace had brought us to an expansive plaza where one would curiously cock their head at the sight of the iron-exposed pyramid of the Louvre if they didn't know what they were looking for. Shayna disrupted my trance, waving me toward her.

"We have three other museums to get to today."

She was rigid with purpose, flashing past the expansive religious pieces from the Renaissance, divine homages that extended the span of the wall from floor to ceiling, in pursuit of the golden goose.

The *Mona Lisa.*

Our pace came to a quick halt, hitting a human wall twenty-feet deep. Some were politely, while others deliberately, pushing through the vacuum-sealed crowd to get as close to the *Mona Lisa* as possible for their moment of selfie fame with the five-hundred-year-old masterpiece.

Suddenly, all of the magic of Paris dissipated into absurdity, earning Shayna her first strike on my personal list.

I told her that I did not want to rush out of here like a cannonball, to which she obliged.

We waltzed out.

Next came the Musee d' Orsay, requiring another trek through the rain across the bridge to the opposite side of the river, dodging toy cars, softened by the plethora of photo-ops to capture the dreary days of slippery Paris. We slid into the renovated railway station, purchasing yet another ticket for a museum one could spend a week in, compared to the hour-long crash tour Shayna was commandeering. This museum's display consisted of a more identifiable assortment than the last, with Monets and Van Goghs. But, having not eaten a significant breakfast, the perils of hunger won out over my desire to actually consume art rather than pass by it. We traded our museum tickets for a table at a nearby bistro.

Shayna was predictable, ordering the French Onion soup to accompany her selfie with Mona before plunging her face back into her phone for directions to our next destination, the Rodin Museum. Meanwhile, I spotted a post on Facebook from Theresa's—

my college roommate who I briefly lived with in San Francisco—
parents who also happened to be in Paris. I immediately messaged
them, jumping at the chance to be reunited with welcomed
companions, which also translated into literal distance away from
Shayna's vulture grasp. They responded, inviting me to join them for
wine and charcuterie later that night.

Oxygen flooded my previously hypoxic brain.

I would finally be doing something Parisian in Paris.

The rest of the day blurred into the mechanized movements of a
children's field trip. Shuffled from this place to that without enough
time to determine how I really felt about anything that had once
stood in front of me. I had grown so accustomed to navigating
through foreign places alone, or by the guide of a local, that Shayna
was ruffling my feathers and causing me to molt. I didn't leave any
room for her to invite herself when I announced that my friends'
parents were here and had invited me to dinner that night. But, she
didn't take it personally. Instead, she happily offered to drop me off
at the hotel while she explored the Christmas markets where she
would wait until I was done.

After my jovial evening of copious wine and ham, I met Shayna
in front of a Hansel and Gretel–inspired stand, where she was
waiting for nougat.

"Tomorrow I have us leaving at six for a tour of Versailles."

Fatigue, laced with wine, prevented any conscious filtration to
take place.

"Cool. But I'm probably not gonna go."

"But it's a historical French landmark!"

"But you have to wake up at six a.m. to make the bus! Yeah, I am
not going."

"Suit yourself."

She emphasized her rejection of my decision with an aggressive
attack of her cementitious nut paste.

"Let's go this way."

She walked ahead, implementing whatever authority remained during the few hours we had left in the day.

The coveted time to get my own lay of the land had arrived. The rain conspired with me, subsiding, allowing me to roam dry and as I pleased. I had no intention of previewing one monument over another. I just wanted to feel the pulse of the city rather than witness the longevity of architecture. Without the interference of my headphones, I allowed my imagination to insert my hypothetical self into a potential version of this place.

> *I am an expat working for a magazine as a travel writer who explores cities in two distinct ways. First, I travel on a budget, using the Couchsurfing.com, gathering guidance from locals. Then, I lavishly review the five-star hotels and luxury attractions, providing two accounts of the same city.*

Wherever this stroll had taken me was barren.

I was on the perimeter of the bustling internal arrondissements, walking by my reflection in the glass-paned doors of endless configurations of apartment buildings arranged shoulder to shoulder. I noticed a plaque out of the corner of my right eye and felt compelled to stop and read.

The residence of Gertrude Stein.

A reminder as to why I didn't need a plan.

I always ended up exactly where I was supposed to be.

I delved deeper into my remote whereabouts, falling into a farmers market that had been clandestinely tucked behind the discreet curve of an alleyway. The market stalls ended in front of a small chapel where a band—composed of senior citizens—was playing a few ditties for the weekend enjoyment of the locals. Snow began to flake down, and people drifted away while the band took a break. Through the parting of distracted bystanders, a pearl had been concealed from sight. An elderly couple lost in one another's arms continued slow dancing to their own music. I could feel the hum of their synchronization. Soft shoeing against the pavement that supported their fragile sway. A band member noticed this and silently waved in the others to play a tune for the lovebirds.

Love and romance had not been recent tenants of my headspace. Yet visceral portraits of the undying exaltation, such as the one before me, made my eyes cloud and my heart impatient. I yearned for that feeling, that embrace, that support of another's arms encompassing the weight of everything I carried on my own.

Tired from eventually making my way to thrift shops, digging through the one-euro sweater bin, and fighting with multiple Parisian waiters to be served lunch as an American, I was ready for my obligatory vacation-afternoon drink. I found a bar with Wi-Fi down the street from the Airbnb when I received an email notification from Ivan.

Ivan was an Airbnb host that had denied my invitation to stay with him during my last two days in Paris. But in his most recent message, sent minutes prior, he invited me to meet for a drink that same evening. He had included the address of the bar, which happened to be around the corner from me.

N ight had fallen, and I was two beers in with Ivan. We had been discussing film, which was also his profession, when Shayna WhatsApped me to inquire as to my whereabouts. I sent her our location, letting her know I was with a friend.

She got there soon after, reaching up to Ivan's face to trade two quick kisses, before taking a seat and clenching a smile. I could tell that she had been eager to tell me all about her day and that my autonomous choice to live my own life was challenging that.

"Do you want a beer?"

"Oh. Um, here?"

"Yeah. Their food is pretty good."

"You already ate?"

I nodded.

"But I thought we were going to dinner?"

"We didn't have plans. You were gone all day."

"Well, I just assumed since it was my last night…"

"You girls need a Parisian to show you the city!" Ivan stepped in to throw a peaceful stone at the tension. "I can take you somewhere to eat and then we can go exploring!"

Two sets of eyes held the anticipation of Shayna's response.

"Okay."

I couldn't believe she had agreed.

"But we have to hurry, because restaurants are going to close in an hour."

Ivan looked at his watch. "Yes, you're right. They do."

Ivan was motioning to stand up when I interrupted him.

"Then why don't you just eat here?"

"Well, I can't eat anything here." She had this way of hiding her bitterness behind a smile without notably altering the inflection in her voice. "It's not vegan."

"Well, we still have some beer left. So it's gonna be a minute."

An inhalation allowed the dust to settle.

"I guess I could just go by myself then."

Ivan didn't miss a beat.

"No. Don't do that." He looked at what remained in his pint and threw it back in one fell swoop. "We'll come with you!"

He got up to approach the waiter and pay before we stepped outside. The figurative cold materialized into a chill off the river bank.

"This is what we'll do. I have wine at my place. We will go pick up a few bottles and then go to the top of Paris to Sacre Couer. There you will see the city the proper way."

I appreciated Ivan including Shayna in our night, but she was not a chameleon that way.

"But I really wanted to take Cee to this restaurant I ate at my first night here."

We were walking up a hill approaching Ivan's flat when I decided that it was time to cut Shayna loose.

"Why don't you just go to your restaurant?"

Her stance became more erect.

"So you want to go?"

"No. *I don't.* I'm not going with you. You're the hungry one. You should go."

The air stiffened.

"Okay. I guess"—it was the long search for words amidst one's habitual reaction to cry in the face of defeat—"I guess I'll go alone."

She sauntered to the curb on the opposite side of the street to look up directions on her phone. Ivan walked over to assist.

"Where are you trying to go?"

"It's this restaurant in the eighth arrondissement called Café Sud."

"You just walk down for about seven minutes and make a left onto Rue d' la Arcade, and it will be on your right," guided Ivan.

"Okay."

She disappeared down the stairs.

We both waited longer than necessary before breaking down the drama.

"Who was that?"

"My roommate."

His eyebrows raised with commiseration. "I am sorry."

"Thanks."

"But now we can do what we want."

"Yes!"

"Wait here."

Ivan disappeared into one of the buildings as I sat in the exhaust of my own fumes, not fully sure how to feel about snapping at Shayna. I could feel guilt on the fringes and remorse trying to climb through the window of my conscience. But there wasn't enough time for me to analyze my behavior. Ivan was rolling up on a Vespa, toting helmets and a picnic basket.

"Are you ready to see Paris?"

They were the magic words that spawned instant absolution of my sins.

I mounted the back of the Vespa, sailing through the poetic Parisian streets, the dew of the day glistening like twilight against nightfall.

Ivan took us to the top of the basilica, where we drank wine and talked about life with the city at our feet.

"I originally couldn't host you because this chick had been living in my place for a month on Airbnb. But she had to leave now. Do you want to stay at my place then?"

Ivan was saving me from what I felt would be a much less synergetic stay with Clarence. And, from what I could tell, he did not expect anything from me besides my company.

"Oh my gosh. Yes! Thank you, Ivan. Thank you!"

I was nervous to find a ripe temperament stewing back at the Airbnb.

But, much to my surprise, I was the first one to return.

My mind geared into hyper-drive, contemplating every possible hypothetical scenario that could explain why she had not gotten home before me. All of them were rendered null since her luggage was still in our room, and the sound of the door opening interrupted my jump to those conclusions.

I sat up on the bed as she turned the corner, grinning from cheek to cheek, an expression she did not abandon after catching my eye.

"Heeeeyyyy!" she cooed, removing her scarf and gloves.

"Heeyy." Preferring not to wait for a delayed explosive reaction, I continued on. "So how was dinner?"

Her response came on the heels of my last word, pivoting so fast to face me that she was almost spinning.

"Soooooo amazing!"

She landed on the edge of the bed on her stomach as if she were auditioning for the role of Sandra Dee.

"The chef came out to sit and drink wine with me after they closed. She remembered me from my first night there."

I was just sitting there, amazed that she wasn't more upset with me.

"Everyone here is so sweet!"

Gag me.

"Well, I'm glad you had a great time."

The ballet on Christmas Eve was a necessary pause between Shayna's highly anticipated departure and changing plans to stay with an unlikely stranger.

Making my way through undiscovered conditions, meeting new people, beholding unfathomable cultural slices of life, and recording new places to memory is a process of will and presence. There are very few chances to sit with oneself and just marvel at the pieces of the whole, because novelty demands our conscious awareness at all times, unlike our ability to daydream in our cars, the redundant rhythm of routine on repeat.

I drifted into an unruffled slumber that night, awoken early by the loud clapping of heels emanating from the floor above Ivan's flat.

Ivan had plans to see his family for Christmas, so I spent the wee hours researching restaurants, all of which were closed for the holiday with the exception of four. Around nine, I called and made a reservation at a French fusion restaurant, walked over for my 10:30 a.m. time slot, and proceeded to engage in the loneliest four-course meal of my life.

The only other patrons dining there were also American tourists, seemingly equally dissatisfied with their Parisian Christmas away from home. I began to write in my journal about the first pangs of longing for my family and our holidays spent together when I received a voicemail. I was not sure how this was possible since I did not have cell service nor did the restaurant have internet. It was a voicemail from Clarence, inviting me to a Christmas get-together he was going to at his American friend's house.

Even though I had canceled my request to stay at his place, I appreciated that he wasn't holding that against me. Unable to endure loneliness on my favorite holiday any longer, I asked an employee if I could borrow their phone. An odd American request that was met with the appropriate confounded Parisian expression.

I called Clarence on the restaurant's landline, unsure whether he would answer from an unknown number and how else we would get in touch if he didn't.

"Hello?"

We decided to meet at Gare du Nord at two p.m.

Once I arrived, however, I realized that we had not specified exactly where we were going to meet within the raucous thunder of the continent's largest train station.

I began to have second thoughts about being in a chaotic hub, alone, to meet a stranger "on his way to a friend's house."

I gave it ten minutes.

If ten minutes went by without us meeting, then I would return to the comfort of Ivan's flat until he came home.

At the very last minute, a man appeared, walking perpendicularly against the crowd, quizzically scrutinizing me, as if to say, *Is that you?*

I walked toward him.

"Cee?"

I shook his hand. "Yes."

"Clarence. Nice to meet you."

He was middle-aged with salt and pepper hair. He was not Parisian and claimed to be British, although he did not possess any remnant of an accent. He came up to my shoulder in height and had a distracting grove of facial hair atop the bridge of his nose. His potent coffee breath prevented me from fully inhaling, pushing my attention instead to his nineteenth-century wardrobe.

He had already bought my ticket, and, without second consideration, I boarded the train.

Not until the train was in motion did it solidify that I had voluntarily entered a situation with no escape.

Pining for relief, I inquired further into his being.

He was an actor, and that's how he had met Clarissa, his friend from California who was hosting the impromptu affair.

That was it.

He needed direct prompting, delivering only concise responses, unable to play conversational catch, driving me into silence. I counted the minutes, watching the city center dissolve into a rural

landscape of gravel roads and slum housing.
People finally had a reason to worry about me.

Thirty minutes later, Clarence motioned to get off at the next
stop.

I disembarked, realizing too late—once again—that I had left any
guarantee of safety back on the train.

"When does the train leave to go back?"

"We have to get on the train by nine p.m. if we want to get back to
the city."

I would not let myself lose track of time.

I followed Clarence's lead past rows of two-story rundown
residential complexes until we stopped in front of a tired unit. My
head was on a swivel, searching for the masked team dressed in
black that was mid-charge toward my direction. I would already be
covered in a burlap sack and tossed into the back of a generic white
van before I realized what had happened.

Clarence pulled out his early generation flip phone right as a
woman—dressed in Russell athletic sweatpants and a red sweater
with holes in it, her hair frizzed out from what seemed to be
electrocution—stomped down the steps, holding trash bags in each
hand.

"Clarissa. I was just calling you."

Clarence did not give any emotive flair to anything he said. What
one would normally inflect with gusto and surprise, he delivered
with echoless monotony.

"Yeah, just go on up. I need a second to myself."

No *Merry Christmas!*

No enthusiastic exchange from either of them.

We made it upstairs and gently opened the door to the apartment.

"Take off your shoes."

"Okay."

"No. She's Buddhist. It's important that you do that."

All of a sudden, a beautiful mulatto girl of about four years ran in and jumped on Clarence.

"Clarence! Clarence!"

He picked her up and kissed her seraphic cheek. I turned toward the direction she had emerged from. Her younger sister—about thirteen months old—was in her mobile carriage, her bare feet moving as fast they could on the tarnished wood floor. As she came closer, there was a noticeable difference between the two girls. The eldest was vibrant, while the youngest did not bounce with the same privilege as her sister. Something was off.

Clarissa returned before I could determine anything else.

"Layla! What did I tell you? We need to be quiet while Daddy is sleeping."

We followed Clarissa into the kitchen while Clarence translated that message for me.

"Clarissa's husband, Franco, works at a nightclub in the city and did not get home until six a.m. last night. So we have to be quiet until he wakes up. Also, he is French."

She shut the door to the kitchen, standing unevenly, pushing out a knotted belly sigh.

"Does anyone want some wine?"

"Me!"

Clarissa opened the fridge, retrieving an already open bottle. She lifted the spoon that was used in lieu of a cork to sniff through the neck.

"It's only a few days old. This should be fine."

She poured two glasses for Clarence and me. I pursed my lips on the first sip and forced a smile.

My family's Christmas is an affair of flowing bottles of previously unopened bottles of wine, cheese and crackers, the Lakers game, wine-induced laughter, and a homemade meal of honey baked ham, au gratin potatoes, green beans, and biscuits. Whatever was currently happening felt like we had inconvenienced the Grinch's ex-wife by our arrival, for which she was shamelessly unprepared.

"So, you guys," Clarissa proceeded. "I didn't get my art therapy done today. Would you mind if we do some?"

Art therapy?

Layla began to jump and chant.

"Can I help? Can I, Mom? Can I draw?"

"Layla! Stop yelling—Daddy's trying to sleep! God!"

Clarence and I stood in the dust of her reaction, awaiting the next move. Layla was unfazed, gently wrapping herself around her mother's leg, infusing her with unconditional love.

Clarissa snapped under the weight.

"Fine—you can. But put on some Sade first."

"Sade! Sade!"

Layla knew exactly where the CD was and placed it in the clock radio player. Clarissa rolled out newspaper as a protective mat atop the dining table before handing each of us a giant piece of white sketch paper and pastels.

"So, what is art therapy?"

"Oh, it's amazing. You just draw what you feel—get it all out. After my girlfriend got divorced, she did it, and it changed her life."

By this time, she had a headband that ran across her forehead. A plastic band supporting a white, upside down, foam triangle that rested in the middle of her brow.

"This is so I won't get wrinkles from staring at the page too long."

We all sat down to our respective posts at the table while Clarissa sat on a small stool with her back to us, painting at her easel. Sade filled the void of small talk until Clarence disrupted the comfort of conversational silence.

"Cee, Clarissa is from California, too."

"Oh yeah? Which part?"

"Northern California."

"Where? I have a friend that lives in San Rafael."

"Yeah. That's it. I lived there in a commune until my parents abandoned me when I was sixteen. Then I said, 'Fuck you guys,' and moved here, to Paris. Met a few guys, got into acting, and that's how I know Clarence. What, it's been like ten years, Clarence?"

Clarence nodded like her obedient minion.

After a while of concocting my abstract piece of pastel eyeballs, Layla disappeared into the pantry.

Clarissa overheard the unmistakable crinkling of a wrapper, her ears perking up like a dog's. Layla emerged, innocently clutching a plastic-wrapped croissant.

"No! You may not have that! Go into the other room and check on your sister!"

I had totally forgotten about the one year old we had left to her own devices in the living room.

Where the fuck am I?

"How am I supposed to parent her?"

I assumed Clarissa had been talking to herself, but she was looking at me.

"Me?"

"Yes. Can you help me? I don't know how to get her to listen."

"Well, I think she was hungry and that's why she got some food for herself to eat. I don't think she wanted to bother you."

"No. You wouldn't understand. She is always bothering me! She always needs something."

I could not talk sense into this woman had I been Gandhi. She did not understand what it meant to be a mother to children, and how could I blame her since she was an abandoned child herself?

"Are you guys hungry?"

It had been two and a half hours since we had arrived, and I hadn't noticed any mouthwatering aromas coming from the stove or oven. I didn't want to be rude, but I was going to be hungry soon.

"Yeah, I could eat."

"I haven't gotten much of this painting done. Could you start the dinner while I finish?"

She meant me.

She wanted me, the guest, to start dinner on her, the host's, behalf.

Considering I had spent the last two hours only drawing eyeballs, I needed a new task to distract my mind from the consideration of jumping out the window.

"Sure."

"Great. Do you see that pumpkin? That's for soup."

She referenced a whole pumpkin—stem, rind, and seeds all intact—on the counter.

"I bought eggs for baked eggs with crème fraiche, so you can use that cupcake pan. And pesto pasta."

"That's quite an array."

"And make sure you *DON'T TOUCH* the pot on the stove! That is Franco's. That is *NOT* for us to eat."

I peered inside the pot.

The steam cleared, and a whole savory chicken atop a bed of rice came into view.

Clearly, she was too tired to do any more food preparation after roasting a whole bird for only one person.

I got right to work without further direction from Clarissa, hacking away at the whole pumpkin and figuring out how to make baked eggs with crème fraiche.

By the time dinner was ready, Franco was awake, and Clarence had accompanied him and the kids in the living room. Clarissa was reverting the art space back to its original form when she came over to the sink.

"Hey. You can't wash dishes like that." Diffusing one of her customary groans. "No. That water's not hot enough."

She was scrubbing away as I stood by when she randomly stopped to look up at me, pausing on my face.

"Hey. Do you wanna smoke?"

I hadn't smoked in a while and considering the way the night had progressed...

"That'd be great."

She was quick to release the dishes back into the sink, consumed by her new mission to gather the ingredients and assemble a spliff.

I had finished both the dishes and setting the table by the time she held her papier-mâché up to the light, examining her handiwork.

Recognizing her exhibition, she quickly collapsed into herself, huddling into a ball before anxiously peering over her shoulder toward the kitchen door.

"Shit. I hope Franco doesn't know what we're up to."

Just then, Layla opened the door.

"Mom. We're going to open presents!"

"Wait! We are cleaning. Be there in five minutes!"

Layla closed the door, and Clarissa got up after her to check it. She came back and leaned against the windowsill next to me, the top half of our bodies dangling in the winter air, holding inhales for a marginal amount of time so as not to cough too loudly.

"I really like you." She stared past the remnants of her exhale before looking at me.

"We should definitely stay in touch after this. It'll be good to hear how the rest of your travels go."

> How did she think this was a bonding moment in our
> relationship? This was not. This was self-medicating.

Before I could feign reciprocated enthusiasm, she aborted the mission, paranoid over her husband's potential awareness of our shenanigans.

L ayla combusted with joy as we entered the scene, cuddling her single Christmas present in her arms.

Her cartoon eyes were glued to Clarissa, waiting for her mom to notice and give her the go-ahead.

"Yeah. Go. Open. But be quick because we have to eat."

Her mother's permission powered her tiny arms to rip as fast as they could, unveiling a generic brand Barbie doll, eliciting a scream.

"Barbie! Barbie!"

She ran around the room fist-pumping her doll into the air, parading around the coveted toy.

In the background, her sister, still in her mobile carrier, was playing with a foam sink brush as a toy. The final, unlikely push that manifested tears.

This was their version of Christmas.

No one was masking their dysfunction beneath formal outfits, too many glasses of wine, and store-bought goods that reflected the financial disparity among relatives. Most everyone I knew operated under the strict social convention to act as normal as possible when surrounded by company, even if it's your own kin. But, here, the facts of the matter operated on the surface; the polarities of Layla's seemingly disproportionate gratitude for only one toy and Franco's stoicism that mirrored that of a gargoyle.

Dysfunction is universal, but we can't accept that in others unless we are willing to admit that we are the same to ourselves.

We all filtered into the kitchen, assuming our seats for our eclectic dinner spread.

I partitioned the plates while Franco sat with the stainless steel vat on his placemat, already pulling apart pieces of his chicken, alternating between feeding himself and feeding it to the baby with his hands.

We sat down to eat, picking at the food that had not been formally blessed or thanked, when Clarissa threw down her fork.

"I cannot eat this!"

I didn't think it was that intolerable considering I had whipped it up in a little over an hour.

"It is cold. Everyone stop eating."

"Clarissa, it's fine."

It was a mild attempt at persuasion considering it was her house, but my tolerance for her outbursts had grown thin.

"No. Stop."

I picked up Clarence, her, and my plates and walked them back to the kitchen. My back was to the table when Franco spoke his first words of the night to Clarissa in French.

"Cee, will you sit down?"

"It's okay. I can do it."

Her tone fell grave. "Listen to me."

I peered over my shoulder. Her expression could not mask the helpless despair in her voice.

Franco was in charge, and she could suffer consequences by not performing her wifely duties.

She and I swapped places to microwave the food. The rest of the meal progressed without conversation.

O nce plates had been cleared, I happened to notice a clock hanging in the kitchen above the door.

8:45 p.m.

I nudged life into Clarence, referencing the clock with a suggestive nod.

"Hey, Clarissa? It's time for us to go."

"But we haven't even had the brownies yet."

"I can't be late," I asserted.

We did not embrace or exchange phone numbers. I left the kitchen to put on my shoes and let myself out.

The cold stroked my cheek, encouraging me to release the residual pain and chaos accrued during a lost amount of time. Clarence emerged, and we walked to the train station, occupying silence until we were securely on the train.

"So, what are you doing for the rest of tonight?" he asked.

"Do not talk to me."

I shielded my chest with my arms, my neck crooked to gaze into the nothingness on the other side of the glass for the final leg of my nightmare of a Christmas.

Solo

The next morning, I left before the sun rose for my train to Amsterdam. This was the only train service I had had with Wi-Fi, so I alerted my next couchsurfing host, Pierre, that I would be arriving soon.

Pierre: *Who is this?*

Me: *It's Cee! The girl from Spain you said you could host for a couple days while I'm visiting Amsterdam.*

Pierre: *Oh, sorry. Yeah. I live in Den Haag. When you arrive, you should take the train to Den Haag Central Station. Really easy. I still think we can have a great time!*

Me: *Okay. I should arrive by noon.*

The train reached Amsterdam, and I remained where I was, anticipating mine being one of the next stops. But Den Haag turned out to be an hour outside Amsterdam.

I had been loitering for ten minutes in an empty train station that resembled a large shipping warehouse when Pierre casually entered pushing his bike.

"Hi."

There was no formal reciprocation of a greeting. Instead, I was pulled into an unwarranted hug. He was tall and Nordic with fair complexion, blonde hair, and blue eyes.

"Um, why did you bring a bike?"

"Because I thought you were a backpacker. Why do you have that huge suitcase?"

This exchange was not playful in the way it had been with Víctor. Rather, Pierre seemed to be from the same distant planet that Clarence belonged to.

"Because this is all I have, and I'm traveling for fourteen days."

"Well, I guess I'll walk my bike then."

His attempts at small talk during our walk washed over me. I scrutinized my surroundings, locating nothing iconic or intriguing about this person or this place.

He suggested we ride his bike around to get the lay of the land, motioning for me to balance my ass on the narrow metal mount above the back wheel. He put on his helmet and mounted the only designated seat while I held on for dear life. My grip froze around the edges and my arms acted as barricades, the single line of safety reinforcements. We only made it to one stop—the Dutch Queen's palace—a place I would have never considered stopping, which is why I requested that we get lunch rather than continuing to tour around.

He made the astute switch from bike to vehicle after our meal because he was running out of time to show me his birthplace.

Yes, the town he was born in.

Our first stop on this personal history tour I had not signed up for was an enclosed pier by the beach. It was akin to an indoor amusement park. Kitschy and rampant with people who had nothing else to do. We wasted an unnecessary amount of time dragging our feet to the end and back before embarking on the hour-long passage to his hometown. By the time we arrived at what resembled a village of gingerbread houses, night had already fallen.

"Fuck. It's dark! You're not gonna be able to see anything."

He was so dumb, I didn't even know how to react. I felt like a hostage on my own vacation, helpless of an alternate route but the budget one I had already chosen.

Our final stop on the extended tour of what no one cares to see when they go to the Netherlands was the most welcomed.

A grocery store.

Yet, despite its familiarity, it only served to validate our dynamic. He was the owner and I was his bitch. He purchased the food he wanted—cheese, bread, and prepackaged meatballs—while I trailed his lead, helpless and shackled.

P ierre plopped himself upon the couch as we entered his flat, not wasting a minute to turn on the TV. I moved in the direction of the kitchen, grateful to have more than twelve inches between us.

"Soooo, are you hungry?"

I waited for the *Friends* laugh track to die down so he could hear what I was saying.

"Starving."

His eyes did not veer from the screen.

So I did what I had grown accustomed to doing in strangers' houses and made dinner.

The meatballs were browning while I cut triangles of cheese when the knife slipped and sliced my thumb open. It was a deep gash that initiated a blood geyser.

Fuck. This could not turn into a trip to the emergency room with Bozo the Clown as my guardian.

I was moving frantically throughout the kitchen, fumbling to turn on the sink and clean it before reaching for a paper towel to subdue the bleeding.

I peered over my shoulder, and there remained Pierre, hypnotized by the television.

"Hey," I said, raising my voice. "I cut myself really badly."

"Oh?"

He did not quiver. He did not rush to the bathroom to grab his first aid kit or make haste whatsoever. I watched as he took his time getting up off the couch, weary of missing what happened in the rerun, to move into the kitchen.

"Let me see."

I lifted off the paper towel that had failed to temper the bleeding. According to what happened next, my method was not as much wrong as it was haphazard.

He ripped two more sheets off, wrapping the dual layer around my thumb, holding it there while stretching to open a nearby drawer. He fumbled around for a few moments before revealing a scotch tape dispenser; the missing link in the mending of my wound. Having successfully resolved the issue, the Dutch MacGyver resumed his sofa spot without a word.

"Thanks."

"Yeah. You should be more careful."

Despite the sturdiness of this homemade bandage, my wound needed rest to clot. I reluctantly abandoned my post to join the *Friends* marathon on the couch. It had not been longer than five seconds when he reached around my back to put his arm around my shoulder.

"Please don't do that."

"Why not? We are friends."

He kept his hand around my shoulder while every inch of my body contracted inward. I tried to focus on anything but his unwelcomed touch. I am not sure how long it was before he retracted his arm to light a bowl, drawing in a massive hit before passing it to me.

"No."

"Are you sure?"

I nodded.

I'm done.
No more of these hooligan festivities I had somehow willingly
gotten myself into.

Each moment inched forward. I craved the protection of my
closed eyes, willing him to overcome his selfish antics with my
telepathic calls that continually went ignored. Drugging himself
further into a sluggish stupor, trading off a bite of food for a scene
on TV, he eventually traipsed into the loft that was six feet behind
the couch and barricaded by four foot walls. I assumed he was
getting ready for bed, so I kept my gaze diverted, finally lying across
the couch, relaxing into a space I could now safely claim as my own.
  "You can sleep in here with me if you want."
  My stomach dropped.
  "Thanks. But I'm good."
  "It's not a big deal."
  He had finally pushed me into last-resort territory.

Pretending like none of this was happening.

  "Other people have done it."
  "I am just going to sleep on the couch like the name says. Thanks."
  I wanted to cry and vomit everywhere.
  My defense sensors were screaming, *Flight! Flight!*, but there was
no way I could leave in the middle of the night with the monstrosity
that was my luggage and a thumb that could develop gangrene. Nor
would sleep become a viable option until he had been snoring for at
least an hour. I spent my impending rest plotting my escape.

I rose with the sun and got ready for the day as quietly as I could.
I grabbed my most valuable belonging—my passport—before
sneaking out to make the train for where I was supposed to be.
Amsterdam.

I arrived before the start of the work day and, in the name of distress, treated myself to Dutch pancakes that were the size of my face. The inviting maze of canals, casual cycling citizens, and pristine waterfront homes with sizable bay windows quickly rendered yesterday irrelevant. In between waiting in line for two hours to walk through Anne Frank's house and the Van Gogh Museum, I imagined myself living in this self-aware city, writing for an international magazine, and hosting weekly dinner parties with distinguished people that could be viewed from the street by nosy tourists like myself.

I did not have Wi-Fi until I finally sat down at a cozy hotel bar I happened on for dinner.

Sitting by the window, glass of red wine in my hand, I checked my phone for the first time that day.

Pierre had WhatsApped me only once.

Pierre: *How are you?*

I let him know that I didn't know when I would return but not to wait up.

How had I fallen into another trap of sheer bad luck with another bizarre host?

I left early the next morning—returning late enough the night prior to avoid interacting with Pierre once more—for Amsterdam's Central Station.

I had an hour to relish my American treats from a table at Starbucks before my train left for Berlin. I sat, distracting myself with people watching, my gaze involuntarily tracking up toward the leviathan of arrivals and departures boards.

My train number was scheduled to leave right then.

I confirmed the number on my printed ticket, which said it wasn't scheduled to leave for another hour. It took a second before my body could respond properly, relinquishing comfort food for the necessary aid of the help desk.

A female agent sat behind the glass ticketing window.

"I am so sorry, but I just noticed that my ticket shows a different time than the board. I think I missed my train."

She took my ticket without any sympathetic interest, redirecting her attention toward the computer.

I stifled tears, justifying her indifference to my emotions with how she could not see the numerous forces I had been battling against. How exhaustion reacts with vulnerability, causing it to boil at the surface and bubble into tears.

She slid me a new ticket and explained in thick, Dutch-filtered English, "Your train now leaves in an hour. When you get to the border and the attendant asks for your ticket, just show them this note that I wrote here."

She mechanically tracked her head back to the computer screen as I turned away, clutching my ticket just as Layla had clutched her doll.

The train to Berlin made multiple stops, lasting well into the night.

Since I had missed my original reservation, I had been downgraded. During the last two hours of the trip, I was one of many passengers without a seat, standing in the aisles or by the doors between cars. Each one of us loiterers employed a different method of diversion: headphones in iPods, sitting on the floor reading, or simply staring into space.

But this disjointed form of travel did not dampen my gratitude. If anything, it amplified my excitement.

I could not wait to see Derek.

Back when I was researching destinations for my trip, alternating between tabs, I scrolled through recent status updates on Facebook.

Derek had just posted:

NYE 2013: BERLIN!

I hadn't seen him since before he graduated two years ago, and a familiar face during my days traveling alone wouldn't be the worst thing. So I asked him if he would mind my tagging along.

Derek: *I'll be with my family, but you should definitely come!*

It wasn't until I began researching where I would stay that I became privy to the avant-garde level of cool that Berlin was associated with: underground music, three-day-long clubbing, and the flagship of street art.

The second auspicious choice—the first being inviting myself to a bohemian city like Berlin—when planning this part of my trip was booking my first ever Airbnb.

I was hours away from redeeming the penance of enduring strange encounters with the timely accompaniment of a trusted friend with whom I could behave as I pleased.

Things were on the edge of shifting.

D erek and I met at a bar to catch up over a beer, but I was anxious for it to only be one.

I was ready to surrender to the night.

Our descent into the subway doubled as the gateway into the underground universe of losing one's mind for an unpredictable amount of time.

We stood waiting for the train.

"Do you know where we're going?"

"Kind of. Not really. I think we're just gonna feel it out."

"Is that a good idea? How do you even know if any of these clubs are good?"

Derek looked like one of those giant inflatable Gumbys in front of car dealerships. The cold had usurped his six-foot-four frame—rubbing his palms together, shoulders wriggling to create friction beneath his coat—making me look like a champ for both enduring the cold better than he and being the easygoing one.

A subway approached. We got on and took two seats.

"Derek. Look. Let's just go to Ritter Butzke first. Or maybe we'll meet someone, and they can explain to you why I'm right."

He rolled his eyes.

At the next stop, a swarm of people our age poured in. Most toted open containers, the serum that fueled the cacophony of the boarding crowd.

Three of these youthful locals took the open seats next to us. Without any reason or prompting, one of the girls turned toward me and smiled.

"Which club are you guys going to tonight?"

I sent a proud smirk in Derek's direction before replying.

"Not sure, but we're thinking about Ritter Butzke."

"That's where we're going!" announced the girl. "You have to come with us. I am Stephanie."

"And I am Eline."

"And I am Sascha."

German friend group to get us into the club: check.

We were successfully admitted only because Sascha had warned us against speaking English in line.

"The bouncers are selective about who they let in. Some nights they let girls in jeans in, some nights not."

Stephanie waited for us beyond the doors of the abandoned three-story warehouse.

"Do you want to stay with me or go with Sascha?"

Derek and I exchanged confused glances.

"He is here to do the drugs, you know?"

Derek and I nodded in synchronization, sharing a reinterpreted glance.

"I'm sorry," Derek began. "I think we will hang out with Sascha for a bit."

We walked deeper into the renovated space. A bar sat closest to the entryway, with a dance floor just beyond it that bled into the DJ stage. Purple lights braiding the fog, emanating from the shadow of the music man's wings, was enough to alter our perception. We pushed through, weaving in and out of other rooms before spotting Sascha in the courtyard.

Derek took the lead.

"Hey!"

"Hey!" he authentically reciprocated.

"Do you mind if we, you know, hang out with you?"

"Fuck yeah!"

Sascha gave us both tight hugs before exclaiming, "It's my twenty-first birthday!"

He threw his hands in the air as we joined in the revelry, offering a chorus of woos all the while anticipating the appearance of the drugs.

Sascha was in the zone. The music had already penetrated his being, and he was lost in the serenade of the beat, a beer somehow still balanced in his slithering hand.

Derek and I loitered beside him, envious of his inhabitance of a land we lay outside of, until Derek broke the fourth wall.

"So, are you taking any drugs tonight?"

"Oh, yeah! Yeah. Yeah."

The American proclivity to exert our property as private—especially our illegal property—made it difficult to interpret what he meant.

"Do you think we could have some?"

Derek looked like a middle schooler trying to convince the leathery curmudgeon in a pick-up truck to buy him a six-pack.

"Of course! Yes! It's my birthday!"

Derek reached into his pocket to pull out some cash.

"Wait. No. No. Put that away."

Sascha dismissed our cultural customs, reaching into his shirt pocket for the button-sized plastic bag. He clandestinely transferred it via a bro-hug to Derek before putting both arms around our necks to form a barricade with our backs.

"Go. Take."

Derek and I dug in with our pinky fingers. The bitterness of powdered e-crystals coated the sobriety of my gums.

I don't remember when time dissolved. Derek and I floating from room to room, separating from and reuniting with Sascha, as infinite appendages of sound. The music dictated our movements. Some shifts asked that we move to a different level for a different beat, others—more literal—funneled through our bodies, stimulating fluid contortions mirroring the constellation of notes. The haze both obscured and heightened our senses. We felt everything and everything was weightless.

We left the club at seven-thirty, exiting into a pale morning empty of harmonic tone or visual sedative. Form concretized. Those moments of ease I thought would never end had passed.

That is the roundness of the drug experience.

The come down.

It was as if we had touched heaven—stunned by the privilege to have the mystery that lies beyond revealed to us—only to densify back into a world we would never see the same. A world void of that divinity we not only had been shown existed, but we had become.

The next time I saw Derek was for New Year's Eve. However, Part II of our Berlin-rendezvous was unforeseeably more frenetic.

Derek and I got separated at a club, because I ended up meeting someone, who I went home with and woke up next to on New Year's Day.

My memory loop of the night before could be condensed into fifteen seconds.

> *Drinking games at a house party with new German friends bled into finishing the rest of Sascha's E en route to a nightclub before arriving at said nightclub and Derek mustering up the courage to approach a random dude for drugs in the bathroom. The random dude being the one who had just gotten out of his bed.*

It felt early.

But there was a subliminal pressure hanging in the air to get up. To dig through the remnants of last night as I searched for my clothes in between sheets and underneath furniture that wasn't mine.

He reappeared in the doorway as I was zipping up my dress, his defined penis lines stalled by his once rolled-over joggers.

"Wow. Has anyone ever told you you have great tits?"

"Uh..."

It was that blushing, caught-off-guard moment where something is said in a way you don't appreciate but you feel like you are being seen nonetheless.

"Thanks."

"So." He didn't sit down next to me or ask me how I had slept. "My friend just called and I totally forgot—I'm getting brunch with his grandmother and him in an hour."

"Okay."

"Yeah. So I really have to get ready."

"Right."

He turned before an afterthought spun him back.

"Oh! Don't forget your friend's coat."

"Huh?"

"Remember? We got coats from the coat check last night? I took his cause I didn't have one?"

I'm such a bad friend.

I just remembered I didn't even tell Derek I was leaving.

"Right. Okay. Thanks."

He got in the shower, and I let myself out.

I realized as I descended the stairs that I had no idea where I was. I turned left out the door without thinking, walking for about five minutes, no familiar landmark in sight, arguing with myself whether or not to go back and ask for directions. I tried retracing my steps, but I couldn't discern his building from the others.

I wandered until I saw a sign advertising *Free Wi-Fi* in a window.

It was a modern diner, empty of patrons. I took a seat at the countertop, frozen in replay of everything that had just happened. The hipster server slid me a menu and poured me a cup of coffee. That guy had been my first one-night stand.

I left Berlin for my final stop in Bruges numb with exhaustion. I arrived at the B&B as breakfast was being served. Since there were such few rooms, I was asked to leave my luggage there and formally check in later once the rooms had been cleaned.

I reemerged into the gloomy, brisk air, bothered by a feeling I'd developed since Germany.

Where do I go?

I had passed by an American-sized bar on the neighboring street during my way in, and although it was ten in the morning, what else is there to do in Belgium besides try beer?

Over my first pint, I considered that I had stretched my trip too long. The beer could not animate me, and my loneliness was at an all-time high. It had been nice to see Derek though. He possessed a rare quality I had been searching for in my relationships.

Mutual respect.

A recurring theme in my life with both strangers and friends had been the unthinkable treatment I'd received from others.

Why are so many humans programmed to be selfish or manipulate others to get what they want?

I did not know the answer beyond that it wasn't only an aspect of Americans or the male species. It was people in general. We are all trying to figure out the proper methods to abide by in this world. Some consider it a formula—tangible and logical—while some believe it to be rooted in tradition; some crave the opposite of the life they were exposed to in childhood, while some just copy the actions of others, perpetuating the lack of respect we not only deny one another but are unequipped to offer ourselves.

I roamed the city aimless and cold. All I could focus on was the number of couples paired up.

Everywhere I turned, men and women were lovingly strolling hand in hand with their significant other. I could have been easily picked out of the crowd as the lone she-wolf crawling across the cobblestone, painfully unaware that Bruges was the second most popular city in the world to be proposed to after Paris.

Continuing along, the new James Bond movie poster advertised at the local movie theatre caught my eye.

I turned around to pop back into a market I had just passed, about a five-minute walk the other way, to buy a baguette and cheese for the show. I returned to the theatre, walking up to the old-fashioned booth, putting my finger up to indicate one.

"James Bond."

He responded with the price in perfect English.

I sheepishly grinned at my idiocy, reaching into my coat pocket for my wallet, but it wasn't there. I felt around other pockets, the grocery bag, trying to mentally soothe my panic, reassuring myself that it was *somewhere around here.* The theatre employee's eyes reflected my own helplessness back at me. I left without explaining my plan to retrace my steps, running back into the street to reexamine every millimeter of exposed ground, indifferent to the likelihood of being stepped on while going against the flow of traffic.

I stormed into the grocery store.

My checker was still manning his post.

"I left my wallet here. Did you find it?"

He did not look up from scanning the items before making direct eye contact with me.

"No."

"Well, can I look?"

He shrugged.

I encroached on the current patron's personal space, frantically examining the area around the credit card scanner, on the floor, and by the bagging station to no avail. I left without saying anything to either the customer whose space I had violated or the apathetic checker.

I ran back to the theatre and did the same thing again, going back into the grocery store and, by the time I returned, the original checker was gone.

I interrupted his replacement.

"Where's the other guy?"

"Oh, he just took his break."

How convenient of him.

I scanned the road back to the theatre for a third time, overwhelmed by defeat. My wallet had everything except my passport: my Spanish ID, my American and Spanish credit cards, and seventy euros in cash. I still had not checked into my hotel and hoped that, at the very least, they would let me sleep there since they had my credit card information on file.

The theatre employee's eyebrows perked up at my arrival through the door. I shook my head, downtrodden.

"I need help."

He sweetly offered a few words of comfort, but my patience was in short supply.

"How do I get to the police station?"

He gave me turn-by-turn directions, but I didn't wait for a final farewell.

I was already sprinting through town. The tourist disrupting the picturesque winter wonderland with hysteria. But I didn't care anymore. I reached the station at rush hour, standing last in the queue behind three other women.

I tried to control my heavy breathing, a sound that was readily apparent against the stolid air of this rigid domain.

I was a jumble of sensations. Half glass full, half glass empty, then this glass is so tired and helpless that tears were spontaneously condensing along the rim.

A vacancy between the desk and myself distilled into view.

I moved forward to greet the officer, shamelessly ignoring his face to peer through the six-inch thick glass. My fifteen-year-old self lay horizontal along the surface of his desk.

"That's me!"

"It is."

"Where did you find it?"

"Someone turned it in."

He collected the strewn cards and returned my wallet.

"Wait—I had seventy euros in here."

"You're going to have to fill out a report, then."

I was taken through the official hallway to sit with a different policeman in his chambers. He was friendly, reaching out to connect with me—his son also lived in Spain—taking advantage of the now rare moment of being a father. I nodded politely in his direction. I was so far past shut down that, although I appeared to be occupying physical space, I was just passing through it.

Americana

Even though I hadn't spoken Spanish in two weeks, my language development had accelerated during its hibernation. I was talking to people without consideration for my own form or logic, and the result was intelligible. Expressing myself without thinking finally made my time spent with others feel mutual. But just as quickly as my occupation of the Spanish philosophy **work to live** got comfortable, everything started to shift.

At first glance, it is common to deduce that life is easier in Spain because it is cheaper, people stay out later, and they regularly cherish the simple pleasures that Americans cannot justify the time to revel in.

As much as I was putting pressure on myself to gain more linguistic and cultural knowledge, I also took the time to bask in the novelty of *pueblo* life.

> *Runs through endless orange groves where not a soul was seen. Lengthy walks alone to the train for yet another weekend getaway. Lunches that extended four hours to simply share one another's company.*

But, with frequency, the novelty wore thin.

The elements of America I had formerly denounced—the tangled web of cars, noise, technology, hustle, money, and status—finally had something to be compared to.

Through the lens of an Orange County microscope, I considered these aspects to be symptoms. But, when placed within the context of the world at large (Spain and snippets of Europe), these symptoms were expressed as strengths. As the reasons people sacrifice everything to pursue a life there. To be overwhelmed with the amount of opportunities and the competition necessary for those opportunities to hold value. To be filled with hope and determination at the prospect of making something of yourself. Not just for your family but for yourself because, in America, you can be anything you want to be and that is the epitome of empowerment.

I would have never thought about how the economic recession was impacting other parts of the world until I had been placed in a Westernized country that was waiting to be rescued from the rubble of the collapse. Helpless citizens would go on weekly strikes instead of going to work. And when employees of the state did not go to work or small shop owners did not open that day, they did not get paid. That money strategically stayed in someone else's pocket. Someone else manipulating the general public with an announcement of civil unity via a weekday strike on the TV. Someone who both held a political seat and owned the media outlets. Someone who controlled the weekly shutdowns because they could capitalize upon it.

I met countless postgraduates my age and older, living at home, without any prospects of a job unless they had both a master's degree and spoke English or German. I could feel the pain they carried in their hearts, shielding it with a smile, withholding their curiosity over someone like me somehow living around someone like them.

So, yes, Spanish people work to live, and it's charming because Americans don't do that. But no matter how much I loved the people I became close with in Peñaflor—no matter how well they treated me, no matter how much of a respite I needed from

American life—Spain was not the nirvana I had hoped it would be.

As the months dwindled, the rare pauses between activities were not peaceful respites as much as they were pending possibilities. Many of my fellow interns from Ranger had followed directly down the agency route after college, working in the mailroom, and climbing the ranks to desk positions as assistants to agents— knowledge of their lives exposed through the luminous portal of Facebook.

I reached out to Gene, the talent agent, informing him that my travels would be ending soon. He responded encouragingly, requesting that I inform him once I returned to American soil to set up a formal meeting then.

It was a minor fist pump of victory, but it couldn't compare to a verbal confirmation of secured future employment. Although I wouldn't trade what I was doing to be sitting behind a desk in Century City, my competitive reflexes were quick to react to other people's success compared to my gypsy wandering.

These states of self-provoked urgency came in waves, broken up by my prophesied friendship with Pilar.

Isabella had begun seriously dating a man in town just as Pilar had begun inviting me everywhere.

Clubbing in Seville. Her beach house in Málaga. The feria alongside her longtime boyfriend and family, clothed in traditional garb, dancing to live acoustic flamenco beneath a caseta filled to the brim with celebration fueled by ribujitos.

I even attended her graduation from undergrad as well as the celebratory dinner with another classmate's family afterwards. On the surface, life could not have been any more perfect.

Language command. Travel. Heart-centered friends. The time and means to exist.

But I was occupying two worlds. The one in my mind and the one in front of me. The one that doesn't exist and the one I am currently in. Although I had accomplished everything I had listed as my goals (and/or manifested), my mind started reminding me that it was only temporary.

Around this same time, I had asked my mom to send me a care package. Tampons, deodorant, homemade granola, Trader Joe's peanut butter, and my neti pot. I had to ask her because she hadn't thought to offer. And, as she left the post office, she called me to ensure that I understood that it had cost forty dollars to ship forty dollars worth of stuff.

The piercing reminder that nothing at home had changed.

Piercing because I hadn't healed. Spain had not been a transference of pain. If anything, it had been a dream. A world that no one else in my waking life had seen and therefore could not imagine. A world with the same elements as my waking life—challenges, emotions, disappointments, lessons, opportunities, and unrivaled bliss—but with the added layer of spectatorship.

No matter whether your teeth get knocked out in a dream and you can't speak or your dog gets sick because you keep forgetting to feed him, you eventually wake up. No matter how tragic life seems in the moment, you don't react as much as you watch it happen until some force stirs you to leave. The image and its attached feelings evaporate as you break back into consciousness.

Freaky Clarence, German Fuckboy, and Pervy Pierre were recent pieces that had evaporated.

Well, kind of.

The hazy obfuscation of my dream world (that was actually my present reality) was not easily decipherable. It wasn't until beginning to edit this, two years after having first written it, that the MeToo movement was in full effect. It wasn't until then that I could see the irreplaceable sediments, scarred and disfigured, that these men's evaporation had left me with. No, I had not been raped or assaulted, happenings that are still shockingly easy to come by within our progressive level of civilization, which makes it difficult for us to understand **the why** and remedy *the what.*

Which is why we react instead.

But, the thing is, I didn't even react to those men. MeToo highlighted how much I had collapsed inward and forgot, and how—I believe—many other women do too when faced with these circumstances. I am not equating what happened to me with sexual violence. But, what I am highlighting is how unprepared we are for unwanted sexual encounters of any sort. How pervasive these moments are and, with repeated exposure, how much we desensitize ourselves to the way they make us feel. How we don't take responsibility for our actions and change them, and how burying prevention beneath hurt and blame is exactly what paves the way for what is to come in LA.

> *I will develop a thick skin to unideal treatment by men*
> *instead of doing something about it, such as changing my*
> *behavior or how I regard myself by not putting myself in*
> *situations with men who only want one thing.*

My dream world has since become this story of a process in and out of pain that I can only now define as an expedition of the soul.

I was not a victim in Spain shedding layers from the past.

I was not the social illusion that the exotic backdrop of travel heals the troubles the rest of us staying in one place are bound to suffer from.

I was in Spain to expand my meaning of what it means to be alive.

I was not in Spain to condemn America.

I was in Spain to understand freedom.

As a sixteen-year-old, freedom was life outside my parents' rules. As an eighteen-year-old, freedom was partying. It was an insulated independence that—with my limited exposure—had been relatively defined as "boundless." I proceeded to spend the following three years praying to be graced with a second chance at freedom. A freedom I would not spoil with shenanigans but honor with gratitude. When, as a twenty-two-year-old, I was free to travel into a situation that would allow me to immerse myself in a literal manifestation of the unknown. A place where *Andalucían* dust would smudge my patriotic blood of its impurities. But only as a twenty-nine-year-old can I truly see that freedom is not a physical state. It is a mentality. A mentality of limitlessness that opens our minds to new ideas, reminding us of the reason we are thrown into the unknown a countless number of times in a single lifetime.

To free *ourselves*.

To free ourselves from everything we think we know.

Travel is simply a vessel into the unknown just like our dreams.

They are our subconscious ways of engaging with the most literal manifestation we have of being present in discomfort. The goal then becomes to lose ourselves to such a degree that we don't know how to describe the world we're inhabiting because of our level of relinquishment. Our level of disassociation with what we thought was going to happen and what is actually happening.

The difficult part is sharing this inner transformation with others. The hard part about letting go of complaints, pain, judgments, and expectations to live in harmony with the present is that we become irrelevant.

We're hyperaware of the surreality. The magical tints that no one will ever appreciate as deeply as we do because they aren't in our bodies. So we ignore the light calling us back into the concrete world through the skins of our eyes as long as we can. We relocate to the last retrievable moment, melting into the weightlessness of our dreams.

Barcelona

I had not scheduled Couchsurfing during the month of February, having reached my fill with the last two faulty experiences.

So, I stayed at my first ever hostel while in Barcelona instead. However, once there, I quickly remembered why I had avoided hostels to begin with.

I arrived late at night during a pre-party gathering. A mixture of beer pong and unprovoked shots from a nondescript kitchen. Despite my multiple claims of assurance that I was fine left to my own devices, the front desk employee insisted on introducing me to the guide of that night's bar hopping tour. Unfortunately for me, her natural Australian ease succeeded in convincing me to at least come out to the first bar. But, just the first bar quickly turned into a club where every patron could be found at one chance or another surveying the party scene for a candidate of their compatible preference to be that evening's drunken mistake.

Every nerve in my body stiffened with resistance to the same environment that ignited my hostel mates' temptation centers. I was forcing myself to interact with people all because someone had invited me; yet, why did someone's invitation mean that I had to accept?

For as much as I would crave human interaction after spending strings of days alone, distantly observing the majority of the inhabitants of the world passing by with someone else, off to work, or to pick up their kids, I knew better than to participate in surface-level interactions such as these with people I did not know.

The hostel guide pulled me out onto the dance floor.

I was mustering the strength to dance despite this club's poor attempts at "sexy vibes," faultily characterized by strobe lights and a black lit bar, inconveniently placed in the center of the room. It wasn't long before two guys approached us and invited us to dance by rubbing their respective crotches against our legs. I obliged, but not without creating the impression that I didn't know what I was doing.

I shifted my weight like sludge in a circular motion, as slowly as possible, before breaking out into spastic dance moves, jumping, flinging my wrists around with goal-post arms, jerking my chest in and out of cat-cow pose. But, instead of dismissing me, he turned me around to face him. He was significantly shorter than I and whispered in my ear.

"Are you American?"

"Yes."

He had a French accent.

"My name is Louis."

"OK."

He was trying to dance with me again, pulling my forehead down to rest against his when, the next thing I knew, Louis had his hand traveling towards the forbidden land down my pants.

"What the fuck?"

Without thinking, I yanked his hand out and stormed off, not bothering to bond with the hostel guide over what had happened. I released myself from the suffocating fog into the crisp night without any idea as to my whereabouts or the desire to convince any unfriendly bouncers to help. I walked as quickly as I could away from this dim network of alleys using the city lights as my North Star. I hailed a cab back to the hostel, hoping to wake up with amnesia concerning the night before.

I began the next day at La Rambla, a large canopied market with an overwhelming selection of fresh meat, fish, cheese, fruit, vegetables, candy, and bread.

Items hung from the rods supporting the tent while vendors—squished side by side—fought for my attention to shop with them from across the walkway, yelling over one another, marketing their goods.

When I traveled, I had devised a method of indulging in a tasty breakfast, a store-bought baguette and cheese for lunch, and investing in a formal culinary experience again during dinner.

My baguette and cheese from one of the stands rested in my purse as I took an audio tour through Gaudí's neo-gothic masterpiece, La Sagrada Familia. I spent almost 3 hours exploring the space to the narration from the headphone speaker describing the significance of the most minute details.

Gaudí scrutinized nature and applied sacred geometry to both the layout and design of this holy space. The interior of the building was enthralling with vibrant colors and wondrous meaning beyond that of a church solely dedicated to serving god. This metacreation had been erected with a reverence to Mother Nature herself.

I ended up stumbling upon a hidden plaza after, taking a seat upon one of the cold, metal, patio chairs outside an Italian café. I easily sank into this inner-sanctum between buildings, writing in my journal without thinking, feelings translating themselves as my pen pushed against the paper.

Barcelona

February 24, 2013

I'm waiting for you.

*You'll see me first. To you, I'm not a puzzle. It's not a game.
We talk like people; fears, passions, daily stresses, irritations,
sorrow, joy, love, god, the universe. You will teach me things
I didn't know existed. I will teach you about food, about
laughter, silliness. I don't take myself seriously. You look
at me and smile. I know you're always thinking about me.
You have been since our eyes connected. But, we disagree
on things. You love me for me. You want to take care of me
because you admire the way I take care of myself. I want to
tell you everything; where I've been, what I thought and how
I felt (and why those two things are different). You argue with
me when you disagree, but we don't dispute. We answer that
question, "Why?"*

*I don't know how, when, or what. I don't know what you
look like, how your voice sounds, what you smell like, your
endearing flaws, your ticks, your wishes, or your history. But
you will walk up and startle me. Your blue eyes tap me on
the shoulder and ask me a question before the words can be
formed by your mouth. I have my guard up. It's been there
permanently for a while.*

I don't care what his eyes said. It's happened
before—don't let down.

"What's your name?" you ask.

"Cee. And yours?"

"I'm (insert name). It's a pleasure meeting you, Cee."

You ask me where I'm from and what I'm doing here.

Such interest in a stranger.

Your intent gaze and lack of interest in sharing about yourself is flattering.

He could just be another enigma.

"So, what are you doing here? If I may..."

You answer. You explain. You smile.

You don't avoid. You don't answer sarcastically. It's more difficult for me to pinpoint you. You don't touch me. You are nervous. You don't do this often. You don't talk like this with anyone. You weren't waiting for me like I've been for you. You saw me and realized something was missing. I've known you've been missing my whole life.

I'm complex and it takes you a while to get used to. I'm picky, but you don't complain. Our first real fight scares me. I don't care about the fights as long as we learn from them. I won't know I love you until you meet my parents.

You are going to change my life.

I love you. Always have and always will.

I continued on a four-hour wandering exploration of the city eventually stumbling into Parc de la Ciutadella.

It was not a pristine space or even particularly colorful, but it suited me. There were multiple fountains with statues dressed in symbiotic moss that spread over the sculptures' physiques stained by time.

Peace settled my heart.

I had never thought about marriage, but this place reminded me of a space I could be wed in. An outdoor venue with character and charm for being what it is.

Closing Ceremonies

M y fellow passengers and I watched the crew assemble the boarding stairs from the tarmac. I had never used this budget airline before, but it was the only carrier offering service from Seville to Rome for my final voyage alone. A sky attendant from the plane waved to the steward manning our line, but before he could announce permission to board, the passengers waiting in front had already exploded into a sprint. The businessman next to me had tucked his briefcase beneath his arm and ran into me during takeoff. I took this incidental nudge as permission to follow his lead, peering behind me.

A stampede of human rhinos clipped my heels.

What the fuck?

I couldn't help but laugh.

Who does this?

I arrived late at night without cell phone service, and my ride was nowhere in sight. Luckily, I had made friends with an international student from Italy on the plane, and he offered me his precious unpaid minutes to call and see when my lifeline would arrive.

When I reached out to Justin—a fellow intern from Ranger—about coming to visit him in Rome, it just so happened that the only dates that worked for us both were when his parents were on holiday in the Côte d'Azur. He offered to let me stay at his place, shrinking an incomprehensibly massive city into a place of refuge.

"Hey," Justin answered in that wary tone, reacting to an unknown number.

"Hey. It's Cee. Where are you?"

"*Bella! Ciao!* So, you will think this is great. I do not have a car. Ha ha. I know. I had to borrow a friend's, but it took a while to start. I am about ten minutes away. See you soon!"

Even though I am sure my Roman host must have surpassed his saturation point of tour guide long ago, he was as congenial as ever, guiding me through his historic city and correcting my poor behavior along the way.

Don't ask for extra cheese on pasta or use a spoon to twirl spaghetti on.

Never eat at restaurants with people standing in front of them recruiting patrons.

To drink a cappuccino or latte after noon is a true American faux pas. Those drinks are considered filling and should be consumed as breakfast only.

It was a special time to be in Rome because it was two days before the Vatican's announcement of the new pope. Vatican City was buzzing with media stands, and pilgrims filled St. Peter's Basilica since the Sistine Chapel was closed for the congregation of cardinals waiting to cast their vote.

It was the only city I had experienced where stimulus waited around every bend. The street performers here didn't feel like beggars (the special breed of gypsies here were responsible for that) but like true virtuosos of their crafts. It was a showcase of human existence. Modern survival cradled within the nest of ancient democracy. Bases of structures from two thousand years ago still intact, remnants of their past heights garnished around them.

Rome knew who it was.

It was complex and messy. It was old and diverse. It was overflowing with people, food, and culture. It did not try to change these aspects outside its control. It did not need to analyze it. After thousands of years, it had somehow mastered being everything at once.

I sent my wishful penny behind my head into the Trevi Fountain with a smile.

I was still riding the crest of this wave of fortune. I could not help but post it to Facebook the instant we had time to stand for an espresso, receiving an immediate comment from one of my high school teachers, Mr. Reynolds.

Mr. Reynolds and I had grown close as group leaders on one of the retreats in high school.

> **Mr. Reynolds:** *Oh my gosh! Helllo! I am making a quick trip to Rome because of the pope. Where are you?*

"Justin! My old teacher is here, too! How crazy is that?"

"Wow! So crazy, Cee!" he smiled sarcastically.

"I have to see him. Is it okay if I see him after dinner?"

"Whatever you want, *bella*."

During dinner, Justin and I caught up on lost time. He had invited me to a reggae concert at the Hollywood Bowl during our internship. We ate figs and prosciutto, got high, and put our arms around the people next to us while Ziggy Marley performed *"Love Is My Religion."* We formed a bond that night. I had surprised him with my maturity, and he had surprised me with his platonic acceptance of our relationship.

I opened up to him about my past plights, the most sensitive still being that about Trevor.

"Why are you so upset with him?"

"Because he led me on."

"No he didn't."

"What?"

"He told you not to get close to him. He told you he couldn't be with you. He told you these things. He let you go rather than leading you on and dragging it out."

I thought about this.

> *I had harbored what I thought was justified resentment toward him, but Justin could see the raw facts much more clearly than I.*

"I guess… "

"You know I am right."

B y the end of the meal, I had consumed a conservative amount of wine before heading out to meet Mr. Reynolds.

I spent my nights in Europe cognizant of not libating to lose control due to the timely warning I had received on my twenty-first birthday. A warning that I couldn't understand then but could only understand now.

During senior year, I was still doing things based on what was easier or more popular. Even though I had said that I didn't agree with that mentality, the collective belief in partying, financial abundance, and working to the point of collapse was more pervasive and powerful than my realizations that countered these. I did not yet know how to isolate these cultural norms as such— much yet resist them—because they were insidiously wrapped around every aspect of life.

I was still viewing life on the surface, and what the surface constantly reflected back at me was my isolation.

From Facebook to the small cohorts of people talking to one another as I walked through campus, I was constantly being shown that no one else was ever alone. So when it came to my twenty-first birthday, I wanted people to be there because that meant something. Not what I did but who I was with. But Lucy and Jen—my friends from childhood who invited me to the M83 concert—didn't show up even though I had been there for both of theirs. It was no wonder then that my subconscious desire to drown out the reminder of those feelings—me showing up for others even though no one shows up for me—led me to a hospital bed. It was no wonder that I blocked it out until now. Until a few weeks before they would both arrive on European soil to join me on a two-week trip through Italy and France prior to my return home.

I made these connections as the fabric of my real world seeped into my dream world, but the greater meaning had not yet been made available to me because neither of these pieces of my past were three-dimensional. They were flat pieces of a puzzle scattered along the floor before having been fit into their corresponding places. Not until each piece had been tried and examined could what was once one-thousand fractions formulate something larger than the pieces themselves.

A three-dimensional image.

The three-dimensional image that I could not yet see was that it wasn't Lucy or Jen's fault that I wound up in a hospital bed. That it didn't matter that they couldn't make it because our friendship couldn't be defined by something like that.

Nor could I see that it wasn't my fault either.

It wasn't that I drank too much or got roofied.

It was a necessary experience that I had yet to transcend.

It was like that intuitive certainty that I shouldn't take the Ranger job without the present knowledge of being able to get a job abroad.

It was like getting accepted to TEACH the day before my first date with Trevor.

It was like my obsession with every moment with Trevor because of my fear that we would end.

A prophecy that was fulfilled.

These were all experiences that I had to have regardless of the pain, doubt, or the realized fear involved.

The first quadrant of the puzzle pieces—representing past experiences—I had completed was born out of an accident.

The non-profit fundraiser.

An indirect event that, on the one hand, reaffirmed my frustration was real when, in actuality, was leading me to accept responsibility for not only my actions but the way those actions make me feel.

Only I can make myself happy.

I had to keep coming back to that quadrant to ingrain this realization within me because not only was it unnatural but no one else was openly interested in pursuing such a deceivingly simple belief. And, each time I return to that first quadrant—whether by choice or the natural currents of time—it's meaning has evolved, revealing deeper layers and a more complex form.

My realization of putting pressure on other things and people to make me happy was deeply connected to my inability to understand how life worked.

I wanted life to make sense.

I wanted something or someone to hold onto.

But the more I sought these ideals, the more life showed me that they were unattainable.

Life is not methodical. It does not occur according to our plans or preferences. It is happening according to a plan none of us can see. A plan that is uniquely tailored to each of our souls to teach us lessons reminding us that we came here to learn about who we are.

I had to end up in a hospital bed because I needed the lesson of alcoholic limits to sink in before going to Europe. I needed Europe to be delayed because I needed to spend months manifesting Trevor and my relationship's fruition, just for the lesson that *no one is here to make me happy* to be reinforced. I needed to go to Europe with bitterness in my heart, to meet others with different perspectives to realize what a blessed existence I have actually led. I had to have close encounters with weirdos to understand that boundaries are not parental cages; rather, they can be beneficial when interacting with strangers. Furthermore, I had to have close encounters with these strangers to intimately understand that many aspects of America aren't unique to my country while others are. I needed to go through the last twenty-two years—emphasizing the pain and confusion—to become who I am. A zigzagged, explosive, and incoherent process that leads to a unique perfection. A process that teaches us about ourselves and how to forgive others. A process that is, at times, a tunnel of darkness and, at others, a spontaneous ray of light that clarifies the pain we endured in the dark. A process that we can choose to numb, deny, and perpetuate by never willing to look at the wounds—the parents, the failed relationships, the harm inflicted upon us or that we've inflicted upon others—*or* that we can embrace, heal, and integrate as purposeful moments that were integral to becoming who we are today.

P eace filled the streets of Rome at night. The spring rain massaged the tired stones that carried me to another reunion on foreign land.

I met Mr. Reynolds and a few of his other friends in town for a glass of wine before he and I left and wandered into a rare situation.

The monumental space of St. Peter's Square was empty.

Mr. Reynolds waved to the media stand on the opposite side of the grand plaza. The fluorescence of representatives working around the clock until the announcement of the new elect felt impious in this reverent of a setting.

Mr. Reynolds jokingly yelled into the holy air.

"Hello! Over here! I'm ready for my interview whenever you are, MSNBC!"

His own impropriety took me aback.

"Will you be here for the inauguration?" I asked.

"Ugh. I wish! I have a flight back tomorrow. Just here for a hot second."

I nodded.

"But this is why I came. I mean they need me. I'm like the American representative of the Catholic Church. They need me here right now."

He had taken a brief break from studying for his theology doctorate at Yale. I appreciated being in his presence because that's what he was. Present. He believed in something sacred, ritualized by the traditions of the church, beheld by the holy men, represented by the pope. I respected his pursuits and his beliefs because, at the end of the day, faith is faith. It is to believe in something bigger than ourselves that guides our daily lives in a way that we cannot always understand, but if we take the time to look closely enough, we can see.

When I got back to the *pueblo*, I had an impromptu late night English lesson with one of my students who had been sick the week before. We met at Hotel Tesoro, where they were broadcasting the announcement of the new pope. I took a seat in the bar, waiting for her to arrive, filling time by checking my Facebook.

Mr. Reynolds's post was the first on my feed.

My flight has been canceled! I get to see the inauguration! #powerofprayer

He had made it happen—or god had.

I scrolled down to another post by him.

It was a clip of Mr. Reynolds' interview with MSNBC.

I promise you.

I could not make this up even if I tried nor could I conceive of Mr. Reynolds manifesting what I had initially regarded as a joke the night before when he waved to the media stand.

Chills ignited my body.

I had seen it.

I had seen god grant Mr. Reynolds what he wanted, the same way the universe had done with Spain and me.

Farewell

Antonia's family threw me a going away party, complete with a poster saying that I would always be in their hearts, a cake that read "**We love you Cee**," and a slideshow with pictures from my Facebook put to music. Isabella and her family were there as well, coming full circle to the first time I had invited myself over just six months prior.

We had all gained something from one another. Something unseen yet palpable. Which is why I don't think anyone cried. It wasn't sorrowful. It was uplifting, with a greater knowing that I would see them again.

I made my rounds like that with Alberto and his family, Pilar and her family, Shayna, and Rodrigo and Lucia. The only group of people left to give my salutations to was my school family.

AKA: Miguel Ángel.

On my last afternoon, the school staff went out to lunch in honor of my departure.

We sat outside on the white plastic patio furniture of a bar, surrounded by other employees engaged in their individual conversations, as Miguel Ángel inquired whether I would return the coming year or not. I had been invited to teach English at a high school in Seville where he happened to live.

"I don't think I can."

"How not!? You are almost one-hundred percent Spanish now."

"It's complicated."

Tears were welling. He waited for me to continue.

"My family is complicated. It's not like here. Here is much simpler. You work to live. Back in America, life is hard. My dad still doesn't have a job; I will return without money or a job. And it's just... We will see."

He smiled at this.

"Okay bokay!"

Miguel Ángel's class had made me cards with beautifully innocent notes written inside. How much I had taught them and how much they would miss me. They drew suns with smiley faces and depictions of me standing in front of the class singing, because whenever it was someone's birthday, we would bring that child to the front, and I would air guitar and sing my broken rendition of *"Birthday"* by the Beatles. The kids went wild for it as I danced around the front of the room, swinging my head around, imitating guitar noises with my mouth. They reveled in the glimpse of a superior's capacity for silliness, while I reveled in their authenticity.

Their gentleness had imprinted on my heart. A heart that had grown significantly since the time I first met them eight months ago.

I was finally crawling out of my nine-month dream. My body was restless from the density of waking life.

As I collected myself, I could recall most of what had happened, but I couldn't feel it. Even though I still didn't know who I was, I was different than who I used to be, and there was only one place where I could fully realize all that that meant.

Home.

Acknowledgments

To my parents

There is a lot we have never talked about. A lot I may never know about you and a lot in here you may have never known about me, but this book was not to remedy that. This book was to reflect these parent-child relationships back to society because I feel like we still don't fully understand them. We gloss over the unresolved pain or the stories that are never told because it feels like we are doing the right thing. That we are protecting our kids from too much information or information that would only worsen things.

I am angry at you in this book because I lack foresight. I want to skip over the hard parts of processing all that our relationship means because it is much easier to blame, hate, and begrudge than it is to compassionately release, forgive, and heal.

I love you both with all my heart and I have always wanted what was best for both of you. That is where the hurt in this book comes from. Not knowing how to help you. Feeling helpless when faced with the challenge of improving circumstances upon your behalf.

Without the intersection and deep embedment of our journeys, none of this would exist. So, thank you for agreeing to be my parents despite all of the pain and tragedy that would come with it. I hope you can look past the surface and into the core of what I am saying via the small snippets of our lives held in the previous pages. We are all imperfect. We are all warriors. None of us are exempt. Now that this is all out in the open, let us find the grace.

To my person
A lump in my throat formed as I typed your title.
You are so much more than anything else I've ever experienced. You are the process. You are the change. You are the grace. You are the pillar. You are my greatest teacher, confidant, safe place, alliance, mirror, heart, and love. Thank you for giving me all of you. For knowingly powering me through this tunnel of art. For holding my hand no matter how much I pulled away. For stroking the poison in my veins until it was absolved by your fingertips of light. Without you, there would be no book; there would be no healing; and there would be a lot less magic.

To a lifelong friend and sister
You are my best friend. I don't know why or how, but you are still one of the few pieces of my existence that mystifies me. That I hold so viscerally dear. That I only want the best for. You read the entirety of this text in its infancy. One of two people to do it and told me you could already see that flabby version on airport bookstore shelves. No matter how loaded a situation, you have always told me what I needed to hear because our hearts are intertwined on a cosmic level. Thank you for lending me the time and friendship I have never known with anyone else.

To my other lifelong friend and sister
The book cover is beyond my comprehension. You also bring a lump to my throat. Your presence is incomparable. Your heart is endless. Your gifts innumerable. I do not understand you either. I do not know how the journey you took as early on as you did softened you more than it hardened. All I know is that I can't imagine not being bound to such an ingenious ray of sun.

To a random beach encounter turned forever guide
You are the embodiment of goodness. You don't even have to try. You just are, which is why I love you. In the darkest of corners, you breathed through the cobwebs, illuminating the creative hump of the spider, encouraging me that I already knew the answer, I just had to look at the situation differently, giving it the proper space and time to reveal the bigger picture, igniting my psyche. Cobwebs are not scary, rather, they are all at once delicate and strong. They are what I strived to depict and decipher. The web of life.

To the bio honors prodigy
Your support means the world to me and always has. I would not be this far without your lack of judgment and your willingness to do whatever you can to help me. I can't believe our paths are still intertwined. Watching you blossom into your own dream has been so pure and precious to me. You have inspired me to never let go. I am forever indebted to your friendship.

To my roommate covered in bees
I don't know what I'd do without you. You're a rock in my life that I desperately need and am shamelessly grateful for. Thank you for your constant love, encouragement, and support regardless of how close we live or how often we talk.

To my next door editor
Thank you. You were a transitory breeze that powered through a latched window in my mind.

To an angel disguised as a chef
You have always been there for me, outstretching a hand covered in blood from an open heart.

To my brother
You are one-of-a-kind. Thank you for never interrupting my malfunctioning mind rants and always making me laugh. I know

the future holds a collaboration for us. This will just keep getting more and more interesting. Thank you for choosing me as your sister. It wouldn't make sense any other way.

To professor & co.,
You proved that goodness still existed at a time when I had lost all hope. I was a shell of a person for a long while—lost, tending to wounds—until your hospitality caught me, nurturing me back to a functional point. Your generosity is the shining example of what I want to be for others. Thank you, thank you, thank you. I told you that one day I would repay you and this is that. You were the scaffolding to my dreams. We made it.

To the lady who mothers my dog's best friend
You were one of my first friends in Encinitas. You took me in and nuzzled me with your cooky personality and warm smile. I now can't imagine a world without your long-winded texts, random flat white run-ins, and pickleball encounters because you fill me up.

To my coffee shop family
You will get to where you want to be. I have come to know each and every one of you, and you all carry a sparkle in your eye of dreams bigger than where you are now. Do not lose the glimmer because if your dreams are true, then they always happen. Thank you for treating me like your counterpart, like an extended part of your work family. You have all made the last couple years brighter, especially on days when everything else seemed dim.

To my best friend's mom
Thank you for offering me a job. You reminded me why I am a writer when I had forgotten. I love you and am so proud to see what your newest endeavor has turned into.

To my dog
You came at the perfect time to show me the stunted parts

that I had yet to integrate. You have brought people into our lives that have become dear friends and irreplaceable teachers. You have never been just a dog. You have always been a divine being I have been gifted the privilege of being close to. Thank you for your magical powers and surreal essence. Life is never dull because of you.

To everyone listed in this book
Thank you. I did my best to change the details without jeopardizing the truth. I know I am repeating myself from the "Awareness" chapter, but this book exists because of our connections. Your life, your journey, and your lessons influenced mine and I would not be the same without the decisions both of us made at the time. I hold you in my heart with love and understanding.

To the donors of LOOSE ENDS
We did it! Thank you for fielding my GoFundMe email and turning it into this concrete guide. I don't have words that can represent what a heartfelt extension like that means. It is the epitome of giving, listening, and being there for others. Please know that whatever I can do for you, as is written here, I will. I will honor you in the same way that you have honored me.

To my lawyer
You waited and waited and waited. You also fielded a random email from a person with no credibility and only grandiose ambition. Thank you for believing in this project and taking the time to make sure it not only happened, but that it happened in the most structurally and legally sound way possible. Because of you, I'm not a hack. I'm an author.

To christian, sharon, and genius musicians
Thank you for seeing me and understanding what it was I intended upon doing. I am so grateful to credit you in this homage to a simpler time.

Cee Hunt

LOOSE ENDS is Cee Hunt's debut memoir;
the first installment of a three-part series
called, "The Evolution of Consciousness,"
that explores the meaning of being alive as a
20-something in today's world. Visit the author
online at www.ceehunt.com.

North Node

Made in the USA
Columbia, SC
15 January 2020